The Virtual Speakers Revolution

Join The New Movement of Communication.

Cover Design: Oleksandra Den
Paperback ISBN: 9798357467614
1st Edition, November 2022

This book is dedicated to my wife Kerrie, for keeping me sane during COVID-19 lockdown, and for somehow staying sane whilst being locked in a house with me.

Contents

Introduction

A Rallying Call

"Good Evening,

The coronavirus is the biggest threat this country has faced for decades – and this country is not alone.

All over the world, we are seeing the devastating impact of this invisible killer. And so tonight I want to update you on the latest steps we are taking to fight the disease and what you can do to help...

...And that's why we have been asking people to stay at home during this pandemic. And though huge numbers are complying - and I thank you all - the time has now come for us all to do more.

From this evening I must give the British people a very simple instruction - you must stay at home...

...That is why people will only be allowed to leave their home for the following very limited purposes...

...But at present there are just no easy options. The way ahead is hard, and it is still true that many lives will sadly be lost...

...Each and every one of us is now obliged to join together to halt the spread of this disease. To protect our NHS and to save many many thousands of lives.

And I know that as they have in the past so many times. The people of this country will rise to that challenge. And we will come through it stronger than ever. We will beat the coronavirus and we will beat it together.

And therefore I urge you at this moment of national emergency to stay at home, protect our NHS and save lives.

Thank you. "[1]

As my wife and I finished watching UK Prime Minister Boris Johnson's announcement, there was a feeling that a big change had just occurred. I missed all the shocking announcements of the 20th Century: two declarations of war against Germany, the assassination of JFK, and the fall of the Berlin Wall. The only comparison I had from my lifetime was President George Bush's address to the Nation after the 9/11 attacks. Whilst that was monumental, I felt that this would prove more pervasive and global in the long run.

A popular comparison in the UK in the first few months of lockdown was to the "Blitz spirit" of WW2. I think the comparisons between COVID-19 and WW2 have been at best hyperbolic and at worst disrespectful: in 1940 people sat in their homes without electricity and with rationed food whilst bombs rained down on them. In 2020, we sat watching Netflix and ordering Deliveroo. Was lockdown difficult? Absolutely. The severing of social connection was a new challenge in particular that affected people in an unprecedented way. There's a reason solitary confinement is the most extreme punishment used in

---

[1] Johnson, B. (2020). https://www.gov.uk/government/speeches/pm-address-to-the-nation-on-coronavirus-23-march-2020. Retrieved 5th February 2022.

prisons. Where I do think the comparison between WW2 and COVID-19 does hold, however, is the significance of the aftermath of these two global experiences.

The changes that occurred after WW2 were astronomical: the rejection of fascism and communism as means of governing; the drive towards ending discrimination of gender, race, and sexuality; and staggering technological advancement. The changes that occur after COVID-19 I believe will be equally widespread and pervasive. Whilst many changes are difficult to predict, the changes that are staring us in the face are revolutions in the way we work and communicate. This revolution is coming whether you want it or not, and only by joining the movement early will you find your place in the new society. Remote work and virtual communication are here to stay and the faster you can adapt to them, the more you will succeed in the new economy.

In the new world that we rebuild together after the pandemic is an abundance of opportunities for you to revolutionise the way you work and communicate. You can travel the world from your office chair. The internet allows you to communicate with over 50% of the world's population through your webcam, imagine what happens when the remaining 3B people enter this playground in the next decade. You can connect with incredible colleagues and clients despite never meeting them in person. Whether you represent a company or organisation or run your own, you can be the frontrunner in a new way of doing things.

This forced mass experiment in going virtual definitely hasn't been smooth sailing though. Although the technology has been here to do it for years, our psychology wasn't in the same state of preparedness. Doing everything virtually can feel awkward, impersonal, and even cold. Many of us weren't trained on how to adapt the work we did to a virtual setting and how to communicate effectively through virtual platforms. If you're someone who has always struggled with technology, then this increased adoption will have been a nightmare for you.

Everything we have needed for this revolution has been sitting in our laps for years. I started to communicate through camera in 2015 when I started my YouTube channel, was one of the earliest people to use Facebook Live when it launched in 2016, and added Zoom to my virtual repertoire in 2018. When lockdown hit, virtual speaking was something I had spent years training for. I changed my business from a physical-dominated model of workshops and keynotes that was exhausting me and ultimately failing to a virtual-dominated model of webinars and broadcasts that energises me and has grown even during these difficult times we are facing. Since the pandemic, I have raised my banner and sounded the trumpets that there is a new way of doing things.

I have seen the tide shift in two short years. The future is hybrid: physical contact will always have its place but virtual communication and remote work are not going back in Pandora's Box. The people who are waiting for everything to "go back to normal" will be not just disappointed but totally off the pace. I believe that outside of industry-specific competencies, virtual speaking will be the most important professional skill to learn this decade. Companies and organisations are woefully short of people who can be engaged through this medium. If you want to have a real impact with your work, you need to be equally comfortable communicating physically and virtually.

This book will share with you five declarations that will ensure you thrive in the new society and economy of the 2020s. You have a chance to jump on a rising tide. There is a new way of doing things and you can be one of the pioneers. The barrier to entry has never been lower, it's time to leap over it. The revolution has begun. Will you join the cause?

Chapter 1

Championing The Cause

If you don't think you can have much of an impact in the virtual revolution, then consider the person who took their phone out of their pocket on 25th May 2020, a few months into the lockdown-enforced move to virtual communication. They didn't even have to speak, what they filmed spoke louder than anything they could've said.

For nine minutes, they filmed George Floyd's murder by four police officers.[2] It was a video that sparked a wave of anguish and activism that hadn't been seen in a long time in race relations not just in the US, but around the world. It was damning evidence of a long-established trend of unarmed African Americans being killed (murdered) by police. Protesters marched the streets; media outlets hosted panels; lawyers built cases and politicians drafted bills. Behind the rush of activity and emotion that followed this event, there is a rational question to ask in the context of this book.

Why did this video have the impact it did?

There are obvious comparisons between the videos taken of Rodney King and George Floyd. Both showed blatant police brutality of a lone black man. Both sparked race protests. Both

---

[2] Hayes, M., Macaya, M., Wagner, M., & Rocha, V. (2021). "Derek Chauvin guilty in death of George Floyd: Live updates". *CNN*. Retrieved April 20, 2022.

resulted in trials against the police officers. Yet the measurable outcomes of both videos display some key differences. The protests in response to Rodney King were limited mainly to Los Angeles. His attackers were acquitted by a jury. No policy was put in place to try to prevent this abuse of power from happening again.

Compare this to the protests that happened in most of the major cities around the world after George Floyd's murder: Berlin, Buenos Aires, Edinburgh, Jerusalem, Johannesburg, Lagos, London, Madrid, Melbourne, Mexico City, Nairobi, Paris, Rio de Janeiro, Taipei, Tokyo, Vancouver and many more. At the time of writing one police officer has been sentenced to 22.5 years for second- and third-degree murder, one has pled guilty to aiding and abetting second-degree manslaughter, and the remaining two are set to be tried for aiding and abetting second-degree murder and second-degree manslaughter. When Joe Biden was elected President later that year he and the Democratic Party put into motion the George Floyd Justice in Policing Act. The act has been passed twice by the US House of Representatives, but it remains deadlocked in the US Senate at the time of writing. In the meantime, Biden has signed an executive order on the second anniversary of Floyd's death to enact some of the measures outlined in the George Floyd Justice in Policing Act.

Sociologists and anthropologists will doubtless point to several credible reasons why the response was stronger and more meaningful to George Floyd than to Rodney King. One of those reasons that would be in line with the theme of this book would undoubtedly be the role of social media.

I didn't learn about the incident through a traditional news channel. I first heard about it when one of my speaker connections did a Facebook Live about it. That I think is one of the key differences that made the response to George Floyd so much more profound. The discourse around it spread faster, wider, and deeper, all because people had the opportunity to communicate about it through virtual mediums.

Of course, the comparison between Rodney King and George Floyd does have its limits. It's not like George Floyd was the only contemporary example of racism in the police. Breonna Taylor, Tamir Rice, and Trayvon Martin are just some of the other high-profile incidents that have sparked outrage, but not the mass outcry that George Floyd did. Why was his injustice different? Again there are plenty of educated people who will have valid theories as to why this was the case, but here's mine.

Three months into the COVID-19 lockdown, the vast majority of us were all sitting at home glued to our devices. The only contact most of us had with the outside world was virtual. Many people were fed up, stressed, and upset at the state of affairs. George Floyd's murder was a spark that hit the tinderbox. People who might have been privately upset now expressed that as public anger. The inertia of some towards racism was broken. More voices than ever before spoke up against the crime. Just as important, more people were listening.

I consider myself a fairly educated person, but I learned as much about race relations that summer as I had in the rest of my formal education. That's because I had access to so many more voices who could tell me about things I was previously unaware of such as white privilege; unconscious bias and institutional racism.

Would George Floyd's murder have had the reaction it had if it hadn't hit the unique zeitgeist created by COVID-19? I'm personally not sure it would have. The circumstances forced upon us at that time showed that communication and change could be enacted through virtual means as much as physical. It is an example of how the way we are connecting and communicating is changing.

Until COVID-19, there was a fixation on physical presence. Swathes of the population worked in towering office blocks, there was a migration to cities to secure the best jobs and we were culturally convinced that sitting at a desk from 9-5 was the most productive means of working. We worked to pay for the expensive real estate we lived in and the transport we used to get to our workplaces

We wouldn't see friends and family living in nearby cities for months as we were "too busy". The weekends got jammed full of chores, commitments, pastimes, and social obligations months in advance. We lost hours of our free time sitting behind the wheel of our car or in the sardine tins of public transport. All of this pumped needless carbon dioxide into our atmosphere.

The means for remote work and virtual communication have existed for decades, but we only embraced the most passive forms of them. Our colleagues pinged emails to our phones on evenings and weekends. We scrolled through our social feeds hitting the like button on our friends' posts. We binged pre-recorded TV shows.

Now it seems we have woken up from the technological daze we have lived in so far this century. Companies aren't going to run massive overheads on office space when most of their workforce can be at home most of the time. Employees aren't going to pay extortionate rent for a cupboard in the city centre nor give up hundreds of hours of life each year commuting. We all want more flexibility and autonomy with our work to pick up the kids from school, go for an afternoon run, engage more in the community and protect our mental health. We can preserve our planet by drastically reducing one key source of our carbon emissions.

That's not to say that this transition will be seamless. This was a forced mass experiment that we hadn't been prepared for. Virtual speaking is essentially being alone in a room and speaking to yourself. Our brains know that is bizarre behaviour. Our brains were built to respond to other humans, lacking that part of the feedback loop is challenging in communication. Furthermore, there are very few role models of good virtual communication. Everyone just copies the monotone, death by PowerPoint approach that plagues the internet every day.

Virtual speaking is not as different from physical speaking as people think, it just requires training in a few key adaptions to feel more comfortable.

Virtual speaking favours the small businesses and solopreneurs, you don't have massive overheads to cover to do your work.

You can reach people in dozens of countries, spread across several timezones, all at the same time, thanks to virtual speaking.

In the future, we will have hybrid workplaces combining the intimacy and practicality of physical with the convenience and accessibility of virtual. People will be less stressed and able to balance their health, career, and families as never before. You will be able to work and communicate with greater ease and impact.

No more sardine subways. No more car log jams. We will save money, time, and the planet. Doesn't that sound like a revolution worth joining?

Chapter 2

The First Activist

The car windows had steamed up so much that you could not see out of them. With the engine extinguished forty-five minutes ago, the interior was rapidly cooling on a cold February day. I was shivering and could not stop crying.

It was Valentine's Day, 2020. Instead of telling my wife how much I loved her, I was telling her that I felt like a fucking failure.

We'd only been married six months but it seemed that cracks were already appearing in our relationship. I was barely home. We'd had two massive arguments that week (both my fault). I had been so preoccupied with work that I had forgotten to get her a Valentine's card. That week I started having panic attacks. The one I was experiencing in the car now was my second in 12 hours.

I was burning the candle at both ends, living an unsustainable lifestyle that was wrecking me and my relationship with my wife. I was barely sleeping; my skin was a mess; my hair was falling out. I was normally cheerful but now I was just snapping at my wife all the time. I was normally calm but now I was getting a tight chest and a sense of doom at the thought of starting the next thing on my endless to-do list.

Oh, did I mention that I was a "motivational speaker"? What a fraud.

What the hell had happened?

To look at me from the outside, you might wonder what I had to be so miserable about. I had just got married to a gorgeous, intelligent, and ambitious woman. I was working as a teacher at one of Scotland's highest-performing schools. I had written two #1 bestselling books, hosted a podcast with listeners in over 50 countries around the world, and travelled the UK delivering motivational speeches and workshops.

However, I was struggling to keep up appearances.

I had been balancing my day job as a teacher and my "side hustle" as an author and speaker for 3 years. It wasn't that being a teacher was bad. I got on with my colleagues and (most!) of the students. I did feel I made a bit of a difference with my contribution. But when I thought of being a teacher for another 3 years, never mind another 30, it just didn't feel like what I was meant to do. When we know something isn't right for us, we sometimes sound silly trying to explain it, but we just feel it in our heart that it's not right, and that feeling in my heart was tightening.

What felt right to me was speaking and being a teacher was a fantastic platform for building a business on the side. I had more free time on weekends and school holidays than in any other profession I could have been involved in. The problem was, that my business wasn't working.

My brand "Author Your Life" was a feast and famine operation. I'd write a book and make some sales. I'd get a speaking gig, then they'd dry up. I'd meet a great client, but then I couldn't find the next one. I was making money but it was never large enough or reliable enough to quit my job as a teacher and take it full time.

Furthermore, I didn't feel like I was working with the type of person I could really help. My message was about starting a new chapter of life and writing a different story for yourself. I wanted to work with people who had overcome adversity and were ready to use that adversity to inspire others through positive outlets like write a book, build a business, or start a charity. If you have read my previous books, that is what I had done after losing my dad to cancer.

Instead, I was attracting people who were really down on their luck. They were having a mental health crisis, they had just been made redundant at work, or they had lost a loved one very recently. They were desperate for help and I was not qualified to provide help for those kinds of trauma. How do you encourage someone to write a book when they lost their child in a car accident two months ago?

In my desperation to build the business, I made the key mistake that so many entrepreneurs make: putting more effort into the wrong thing. Author Your Life, sadly, had not proven itself to be a viable option for a full-time business where I felt I was making an impact and making enough money to do it full-time.

So I began to stretch myself thinner. I was getting up at 5am to go to the gym and film videos before I started work at school. My evenings were spent meeting people for coffee, attending networking events, being a guest speaker, or working in the home office up to 9pm.

My weekends and school holidays were spent travelling to cities around the UK where I hired out rooms and hosted workshops at my own expense and put myself under enormous pressure to make the money back by selling books, advanced workshops, and 1-1 coaching. There were plenty of times I didn't make the money back, but I fooled myself with the occasions where I made a tidy profit.

My greatest strength is that when I set my mind to something, I don't stop until I get it done. All my external accolades and achievements in life have come because of this relentless determination. Like most superheroes though, my greatest strength is my greatest weakness.

I didn't know when to quit. I was so blinded by my short-term drive that I failed to see the long-term vision. I needed to rethink what I was doing because I was moonlighting on a failing business and it was only so long before I would feel the consequences of that mistake.

The start of 2020 saw that destiny come to fruition. After a hectic January running a Hail Mary attempt to capture the zeitgeist of a new year and a new decade, the burnout came that Valentine's Day.

My wife and I had agreed to a date to bury the hatchet and try and move on from our conflict that week. But I screwed things up again by having a total breakdown. I uttered aloud for the first time that I felt I was a failure, that I knew my business was a failure, and I was worried our marriage was going to be my next failure.

We ended up not going on that date, but instead, we sat at our dining room table and made a plan.

In the short term, I knew that I needed to get therapy to talk through my immediate anxiety, but also explore my deeper feelings of inadequacy and the pathological pursuit of achievement that came from that.

My wife also supported me to realise that I couldn't stay in a job that didn't feel right for me, and helped develop an exit plan that would provide space to work out the next step and stop my exhausting moonlighting.

I also admitted I couldn't keep pumping fuel into the leaky tank of my business. I needed something more sustainable and more fulfilling.

It took a couple of weeks but by the end of February, we had created an exit plan. I was going to leave the school in the summer and enrol in a Master's degree in the autumn. Being back at university would open me up to new thinking, new interactions, and new opportunities, as well as give me the chance to test something that I thought might be a more rewarding avenue for me: teaching public speaking.

Sometimes life doesn't give you what you want, but it gives you what you need.

At the same time that we were putting finishing touches on this plan, a new word was entering the public discourse: COVID-19. When I sat down with my therapist for the first time at the beginning of March, she said we might have to do our future sessions online. At school, we had a full staff meeting outlining protocols for what to do if anyone should get symptoms. On Friday the 13th of March, 2020, I collected a reference from my superior for my university application, chatted nonchalantly with a few of my colleagues about my plans for the weekend, and walked out of the building unaware that I had just worked my last day as a teacher.

My wife returned from a work trip with COVID-19 symptoms. I was required to isolate myself with her. A week later, the school closed. Ten days later, we went into national lockdown.

I recognise that my experience of lockdown, as it goes, was extraordinarily privileged. My wife and I never lost our household income. I know that millions of households in the UK alone did and are still experiencing the effects of the resulting recession. My wife was not seriously ill with what did appear to be COVID. It wasn't until March 2022 that I caught COVID, and it was much milder than it would've been thanks to the vaccines. We were not in a vulnerable group that spent every day fearing for their lives, or who did end up losing their lives due to the virus. No one close to us has died. Again there are so many who did lose loved ones and weren't even able to attend their funeral. My wife and I do not have kids. We were not trying to entertain and educate children as well as do our full time jobs.

Lockdown did change my circumstances from how they had been a month prior. Whereas I had been burning out and experiencing relationship problems, suddenly I had a lot more free time for myself and a lot more time with my wife. This created some space for me to start working on a new direction.

I was fortunate that our council decided to pay us our full salary during the lockdown, aware that the priority was to get students back to school and that if anyone was going to be back at work in the next couple of months, it would be us. I suspected that I would not be returning to the school before the summer, it seemed that we had gone into lockdown too late and it would be the start of the Scottish academic year in August when students would return (I was correct). I figured I, therefore, had about five months to try and replace as much of my income as a teacher as I could. Then I would have a year at university where my student loan would supplement whatever income I had managed to build in that time.

Already, I was starting to see other speakers in the industry going into meltdown. Their speaking gigs had been cancelled overnight and their calendar was empty. I started advising them. Were they communicating with their audience in real-time using Facebook Live? Were they building a library of content on YouTube that people could watch during the lockdown? Did they know that they could host webinars and virtual workshops using Zoom? These tools that I had been using for years seemed revolutionary to some of them. I also learned that what I had considered rudimentary knowledge such as "look at the camera", was arcane wisdom to most of the speakers who had only ever delivered their speeches offline.

Realising there was a need to educate people on how to communicate virtually, I set up a Facebook Group "Rise and Inspire Speakers" on the 1st of April, 2020. The date seemed darkly appropriate, at that time it seemed that everyone was hoping they were living in one big April Fools joke. With such a challenging situation to confront, I wanted to provide a space to support people and keep their spirits up as best as possible. I was very concerned about the effects of loneliness in particular and I wanted to ensure that people who were isolating alone had somewhere were they could stay connected to people.

The vision for the group originally was to bring together my network of speakers to have a space to support each other and share tips on how to work effectively during the pandemic.

What actually happened was far better than I had expected. The people who joined the group weren't established speakers, they were aspiring speakers. They were individuals with inspiring stories and messages that they wanted to share during this difficult time but didn't know how.

As I started to see the people coming into the group, I saw the clients that I had always wanted to work with. People who, yes had been through some tough experiences, but were in a better headspace and a little further along in their trauma journey. They weren't in the survival mode that we all get in when we have a challenging situation in our lives. They were ready to speak about their difficult experiences and try and use some of the lessons they had learned to help others.

I started to run webinars and workshops for the group. I established our first group coaching program in May, and it was in that program that I got the opportunity to work with some amazing people who made me feel like I was finally making a difference with my work.

Clients like Sara, who came into our group having never told anyone beyond her close family that she is bipolar. Within months she was broadcasting it to the hundreds of members in our group and filmed her first viral video with a frank discussion about her suicide attempts and how to save someone who might be considering taking their own life.

Clients like Raychel, who spent sixty years living as a man before realising that she was a woman. After years of living as someone she wasn't, she wanted to use speaking to help her better express who she really is. Raychel has gained the confidence to start writing her memoir about her experiences as a trans woman.

Clients like Lisa, a proud mum who has spent years putting her kids first and is now ready to start devoting time to her dreams and aspirations to be a successful author, speaker, and podcaster on the topic of joy. Lisa has ditched the crutches of scripts and slides that she used to rely on to speak and is now getting hired to deliver speeches and workshops on joy.

I received requests to speak that excited me and I can deliver from the comfort of my own home. On a Saturday in February I watched a Scotland vs France rugby match in the afternoon before beaming in that evening to speak on a panel at an Influencer Expo in New York. On a Wednesday in August I delivered a corporate workshop for a company in Copenhagen. There was a rare heatwave in Scotland so I was wearing a dress shirt for the camera with shorts and bare feet below to stay professional and cool at the same time. After years of spending money to hire a room in distant cities and spending an exhausting day on trains, I now get to travel the world from my home office. That's what work-life balance means to me.

I published another book in February 2021 "Rise and Inspire: Find Your Voice, Tell Your Story and Share Your Message as a Speaker". It became my third #1 Amazon bestseller.

I received virtual therapy for a year and my therapist helped me work through how I had gotten into such a mess at the start of 2020. There's a shout-out to her in the acknowledgements section as I can't do her justice in this chapter. I completed my Master's Degree virtually, and observed that many of the lecturers could have used some of my tips for making their virtual classes more engaging!

As we emerge from the worst of the COVID-19 pandemic, I see far more of my wife and friends than I did before, I take days off during the week to hike my beautiful home country of Scotland. My wife and I wake at 0800 and I'm usually finished work by 1700 unless I have an evening call or workshop for my North American cousins. No more of these gruelling 0500-2100 days.

As I said earlier, I understand that my experience of lockdown is not representative of the majority of people. I don't want to sound like I'm "glad" COVID happened or smug that I had a successful outcome. I ended up having nearly eighteen months of runway to build a new business and a new life for myself that I recognise very few other people would have had. There is a lot of sheer dumb luck in how my experience of COVID mapped out. Even as COVID-19 is starting to be put behind us, I recognise I still have opportunities and privileges that others don't have. Everything we go on to talk about in this book does have to be set against that backdrop.

What I will say is that virtual speaking gave me my life back. COVID didn't have to happen for me to discover that, but it just happened to be the zeitgeist in which I discovered it. Virtual speaking saved my health, it saved my dreams, and it saved my marriage. The title of this book "Virtual Speakers Revolution" might sound hyperbolic, but virtual speaking really has revolutionised my life. I am the first activist in this new cause, and in this book, I want to show you how much virtual speaking can change your life too.

Chapter 3

Growing The Movement

On the 6th of April, 2020, a man walked in his garden. It was three weeks into national lockdown and that was pretty much all he was allowed to do. As a 99-year-old, he certainly had to protect himself from the virus by staying at home.

This man was not just finding a way to amuse himself during the stay-at-home restrictions. This was Captain Tom Moore, who despite serving the country during one of its greatest crises, WW2, still felt he had more to give.

With his 100th birthday approaching, Captain Moore wanted to walk 100 lengths of his 25m-long garden (10 lengths per day) to raise £1,000 ($1350) for the UK National Health Service (NHS).

The sight of this WW2 veteran using his walking frame to make a determined march down his garden sparked a sense of national pride and cohesion. The target of £1000 was hit in four days. Then £5000 was raised. Then £500,000. By the time "Captain Tom" (as he was affectionately called by the public) turned 100 on the 30th of April, over £30 million had been raised. It smashed the previous record of £5M raised on Justgiving.com.

Captain Tom's efforts continued as he collaborated on a charity song "You'll Never Walk Alone" that reached #1 in the

UK charts, making him the oldest artist to have a UK #1. He made numerous appearances on national television to ask for more donations and he even joined Twitter! A flurry of accolades was bestowed to Captain Tom, the most notable becoming "Sir Captain Tom Moore" in June.

When I need a pep talk, I remind myself that if a 99-year-old can get off his backside to raise £30M, what's my excuse?

The more serious point that I have to raise is that revolutions start with small acts. Walking ten lengths of your garden today might not seem like much, but that didn't stop Captain Tom. He thought ten lengths was better than nothing and that £1,000 was better than nothing. His small act inspired others to contribute their small acts of donations, which accumulated into something bigger.

Your voice in the Virtual Speakers Revolution is only a small one, but that doesn't mean that it can't spark a rousing chorus. There is a choir of messengers waiting to burst into song if you sing the first note. Your small act is what people around the world are waiting for.

I know that this small act takes courage and is something that you may not feel prepared for. Why should your voice be any more meaningful in the cacophony of voices already nattering in the virtual space? I know you have doubts about your ability to communicate successfully online.

You feel awkward on camera. Your imperfections and insecurities about yourself seem to multiply when captured on film: the way your voice sounds; the way your skin looks; how you hold yourself; what you do with your hands; the expressions on your face. Speaking on camera is not natural and it's certainly something we've never been taught how to do.

You worry about your content not being interesting or engaging. You know you rely too much on slides. You feel you drone on in monotone. You think your subject matter should be more exciting but you can't think of how to spice it up. You wonder how people are supposed to buy into what you're saying when you don't even sound like you buy into it. Unfortunately, we've been mired in the swamp of bloated meetings and death by PowerPoint so much online that we have lost sight of the beautiful landscape that attracted us to our work in the first place.

The thing you probably miss most in the virtual world is the feeling of human connection. You can't hug pixels. You can't hear laughter when "mute all" is on. You can't have a spontaneous conversation when there are fifty people on a call at once. When you speak you can't always see people nodding in agreement, writing down a hard-hitting soundbite, or smiling to tell you silently "great job". No matter how advanced technology gets, there are some aspects of human connection that it can only replace, not replicate.

There are certainly challenges to overcome in the virtual speaking space, but no great revolution took place in comfort. We can't say to ourselves "this virtual speaking malarky is a bit awkward, so I'm not going to bother". When Captain Tom heard that war had been declared on Nazi Germany, did he say "this fighting fascism is quite tough, I'm just going to stay at home and let someone else do it" or when he heard eighty-one years later that the country was put into national lockdown did he think "raising money is a bit inconvenient for me, I'm going to stay in the house and let someone else do it"? Our insecurities about communicating online pale in comparison to some of the noble struggles that have been undertaken in the past.

Know that you are not alone in this Revolution. This is something that has been thrust on all of us. We have all had to adapt. We have all had to learn new ways of doing things. We have all had our lack of training or experience exposed. This book is going to guide you and help you through the process of thriving in the Virtual Speakers Revolution. Our movement is based upon five key declarations.

Declaration One: Build Your Movement

You will learn how to build the key foundations of Virtual Speaking so that you can nurture the right skills, get to grips with the tech, and build a training regime for yourself.

Declaration Two: Be Charismatic On Camera

You will learn how to make the camera your friend so that you feel comfortable, look confident and express yourself authentically when virtual speaking.

Declaration Three: Thrive On Live

You will learn how to broadcast yourself live on various social media platforms so that your audience perceives you as more approachable and you can connect with them in real-time.

Declaration Four: Be YOU-nique On YouTube

You will learn how to utilise the biggest video platform in the world to nurture a consistent fan base, attract new audiences and build a reoccurring revenue stream.

Declaration Five: Get Zappy With Zoom

You will learn how to use the most popular meeting software so that you can run advanced speaking events such as workshops to improve client relationships, position yourself as an authority on your topic, and impact people's lives across the world.

Viva La Revolution! It's time to begin.

Declaration One

Build Your Movement

In May 2020, an elderly gentleman is sitting in his basement. Like many others of his generation, he has been forced to come to terms with the technology required to keep in touch with people virtually during lockdown. He is on a call just now.

There doesn't seem to be very much remarkable about this situation. Although the background is blurred, you can see that the man has an elegant bookcase behind him, suggesting he is well read. He sits with his hands clasped and gazes intently at the other person in this virtual conversation, nodding along. On the other end of the call is a young woman talking about her experiences as a first responder. It looks like a loving grandfather staying in touch with his grandchildren as he isolates himself in his home to protect himself from COVID-19.

There is little in this picture to suggest that in just six months, over 81 million people will vote for this elderly gentleman to become President of the United States, surpassing the previous record of 69 million set by the man he served as Vice President to, Barack Obama.

Joe Biden's presidential campaign for 2020 did not get off to a good start. Even before the pandemic, he was struggling. The first three states to vote in the Democratic primaries were won by his rivals Peter Buttigieg and Bernie Sanders. In New

Hampshire, he came an embarrassing 5th place and it seemed his campaign might be over before it had even begun. However, on February 29th, 2020, he rallied in the fourth state to vote, South Carolina, with a landslide victory. Then on the 3rd of March, he won 10 out of 15 states on "Super Tuesday" and became the forerunner for the Democratic nomination.

Lockdown came into force just a few weeks later, but Biden had built enough momentum to finish the first part of his campaign successfully. On 13th of April, he had a live-streamed discussion with his closest rival Bernie Sanders, who gave him his official endorsement for President.[3]

Biden was now the presumptive, but not yet confirmed nominee. This combined with the pandemic left him in a bit of limbo, as it was now difficult to move to the next stage of campaigning.

This is where the basement campaign grew from. Biden and his team used all the virtual tools they could to start spreading their message and building a connection. Biden learned from his slow start. Early in the Democratic primaries, Pete Buttigieg had been performing well, winning Iowa and finishing a close second in New Hampshire. Buttigieg's campaign had used "Stan" (online fan) groups effectively and Biden's team adopted this tactic to support and promote Stan accounts that were favourable to Biden and the Democrats. Additionally, rather than the traditional boiler room campaign calls, they used "check-in" calls to try and get feedback from everyday voters on what they were struggling with during the pandemic.[4] The emphasis was

---

[3] https://edition.cnn.com/2020/04/13/politics/bernie-sanders-endorses-joe-biden/index.html. Retrieved 14th June 2022

[4] "How Joe Biden runs his presidential campaign from his basement". *CBS News*. https://youtu.be/MlqO0r8pvng. Retrieved 12th May 2022

on connection and trying to develop an emphatic approach that would contrast with the bombastic style of the President he was aiming to replace, Donald Trump.

Liz Smith of the New York Times[5] noted that there was an advantage to beaming into places virtually rather than flying around. It allowed Biden to attend many more events and interviews. He ran 20+ surrogate events with fellow Democrats such as Andrew Yang and Hilary Clinton. He was able to connect with local media when normally he would have only been able to hit the big stations. He was even calling voters 1-1. This gave his campaign a grassroots feel very similar to the successful campaign he was a part of in 2008 with Barack Obama.

The flagship events of a Presidential Election year are the Democratic National Committee (DNC) and Republican National Committee (RNC). Both, for the first time, had to be held largely virtually due to the Pandemic. The DNC was hosted in Milwaukee and Biden was confirmed as the Presidential nominee and Kamala Harris as the Vice Presidential nominee. Biden and Harris, however, both made their speeches at the convention from Delaware.

A major difference in this year's conventions was the length of television time, normally the staple media for broadcasting these events. In the past 24hr news channels had a continuous live stream of the event. This time, only two hours per night were broadcast on cable news channels but some of the biggest stations (Fox, ABC, CBS, NBC) broadcast just one. What was more telling was that the stream was broadcast outside of traditional media, with livestreams being available on YouTube,

[5] Smith, L. (2020) "How Joe Biden can beat Trump from his basement": https://www.nytimes.com/2020/05/07/opinion/joe-biden-trump-2020.html?smtyp=cur&smid=tw-nytopinion. Retrieved 16th June 2022.

Facebook, Twitter, Amazon Prime, Apple TV, and many other big internet media companies. Additionally, many prominent politicians and celebrities hosted "watch parties" using these live streams.

The Biden Campaign of 2020 represented a big shift in how Presidential campaigns were conducted. The virtual technology that was used firstly out of necessity then revealed new and more effective ways to reach voters. It allowed access on a more local than national level and may have proven the difference come November.

The 2020 election had the highest voter turnout since 1900.[6] Biden's 80M votes and Trump's 74M both surpassed the previous record of 69.5M set by Obama in 2008. To put that record into scale, 69.5M is like every man, woman and child in the UK voting for Obama. Trump surpassed that by the population of Wales and N.Ireland put together and Biden surpassed that by the population of London. There are many reasons why both candidates collected so many votes. COVID played a big part in making people care more about this election, one way or the other. The ease and prominence of postal voting favoured the Biden campaign.[7]

I would argue that all the virtual outreach from the basement all those months ago was a key factor too. Trump won in 2016 thanks to 70,000 votes in three battleground "rust belt" states: Wisconsin, Michigan, and Pennsylvania. 70,000 is less than the capacity of some football stadiums. Biden managed to win back these states and also claimed Georgia and Arizona.

---

[6] Park, A. (2020). "2020 Voter Turnout Was the Highest the U.S. Has Seen in Over a Century". *Marie Claire*.

[7] "The 2020 voting experience: Coronavirus, mail concerns factored into deciding how to vote". *Pew Research Center - U.S. Politics & Policy*. November 20, 2020. Retrieved June 28, 2022.

In the three closest states (Wisconsin, Georgia, and Arizona) Biden's total majority was just 43,000 votes. 43,000 votes is like American Samoa deciding who the next President will be. Even though hundreds of millions of votes were cast, it was these thousands that were the pivotal ones.[8] Did Biden's emphasis on building connection and rapport at more local levels sway these votes for him? I think you might guess my answer.

The 2020 Biden: Harris campaign shows that virtual communication is vital even for US Presidents and arguably swung Biden the election. I often hear the argument made that virtual communication is not as personal and intimate as physical communication. Of course, that's true. But I would counter that virtual communication is better than no communication at all.

Would Biden have been able to visit a city in all 50 states during his campaign? Possibly. But could he have sat in local radio studios in Wausau, Wisconsin, and Kingman, Arizona on the same day? Could he have knocked on the doors of individual voters in Carrolton, Georgia; Lansing, Michigan; and Butler, Pennsylvania on the same day? These places were where the votes mattered and that was who Biden needed to reach. Virtual speaking allowed him to connect with the voters who could put him in the White House.

Physical communication will always limit who you can reach. This is a key mistake I made when I first started as a speaker. Running regular workshops in Glasgow, Edinburgh, and Manchester was nice, but it limited me to working mainly with people who lived in just three cities. Since shifting to virtual speaking I have had clients in Estonia, Kenya, and Israel. These

---

[8] Lozada, C. (2021). "Joe Biden won the presidency by making the most of his lucky breaks". *The Washington Post*. Retrieved July 5, 2022.

are countries that I have never set foot in and I might go my whole life having never visited these countries. Would I have had the opportunity to work with people this far afield without virtual communication?

This first declaration is all about starting to build a solid virtual speaking foundation for yourself. To give yourself the skills and opportunities to reach people around the world with your work and message.

Chapter 4

Troubleshooting The Tech

A camera and an internet connection. Everything else is procrastination. I'm tempted to just leave this chapter there. People get so worked up about not having the right "tech" for filming videos. This was maybe true in the 2000s when you did need to invest in some proper cameras and lighting to be able to film a functional video. Nowadays your phone films in HD or better and even the webcam isn't too far behind. I know for a fact that you have a computer, phone, and internet connection. You wouldn't be reading this book otherwise.

One of the first things that hold people back from embracing the Virtual Speakers Revolution is a fear of the tech. I'm going to dispel that fear by running through your standard requirements, the bare basics you need to be a successful virtual speaker (it is less than you think). I'll also share some optional extras, and I really can't emphasise enough that they are optional until you have been filming videos for YEARS.

Standard Requirement Option #1: Webcam

I'm sure you've grown pretty familiar with your webcam during COVID times. It's probably been your first introduction to the world of virtual speaking. As you've experienced, it serves the needs fairly well.

I first started recording videos on the webcam. At the time I just used the default video recording app that came with my Mac. If I was starting over again today, I would use Zoom as it's more user-friendly.

To film videos using your webcam, download the free Zoom app and start a meeting with just yourself. Press Record and speak into the camera. When you've finished speaking, stop recording and close the meeting. Your recording will take a minute or two to process, depending on how long you spoke and how fast your internet connection is. Then you will have a raw video file that you can post straight away, or edit (optional!). We'll cover this in more detail in Declaration Five.

Standard Requirement Option #2: Phone

The alternative to your webcam is your phone. What's the difference? The advantages of the phone are that you can film straight into the phone using the camera app, and you don't need to use something like Zoom to capture the video. The phone also has better quality, particularly if you are using the stronger back cameras.

The disadvantages are that you often need to get your video from your phone onto your computer if you want to edit it (trying to edit a video on your phone is not worth the hassle!). If you don't need to edit, this isn't so much of an issue as most social media allow you to upload a video straight from your phone onto the platform. Additionally, it's hard to hold a phone for a long time to speak into it, whereas a webcam doesn't require being held. This disadvantage can be avoided by investing in a tripod to hold your phone (let me stress again, this is optional!).

Out of the two options, I have more of a preference for the phone. The camera is stronger, I can film whilst out and about, I have a tripod and halo light for great indoor filming and I can transfer videos very easily from my iPhone to MacBook thanks to the Apple Airdrop function (more on this in a moment). Nevertheless, I still think the webcam is a great option. I recorded an entire online course "Get Zappy with Zoom" using Zoom and the webcam to prove the point that that is all you need. If you are recording a presentation with slides or talking over a screen share, you also need to use the webcam for that.

Probable Requirement: Video Editing Software

I don't want to freak you out with this suggestion. Talking about editing videos is exactly the type of "tech" barrier that stops people from shooting videos. Let me stress that you don't need video editing to film videos. Most of the editing I do on my videos nowadays is still just clipping the little bit of dead air at the start and end of videos off before uploading, if there is any at all. But you don't even have to do that. If you are quick on the record button or use a timer function, you can start speaking as soon as the recording starts and turn off the recording as soon as you finish speaking. Even if there is a couple of seconds of silence bookmarking your video, it's not that big a deal. On a live broadcast, you don't have that editing function so people are used to seeing that little bit of a transition time on either side of your video. In the beginning, just press record, speak, stop record, and upload that raw video file. Don't worry about editing.

At some point, I do think you are going to have to develop a basic understanding of video editing. Even just that ability to crop the dead air off either end is handy. I know that some people also take comfort from knowing that if they forgot something during their speech, say something wrong or go off on a tangent, they can tidy it up with an edit.

I'll be honest and say that this process is FAR easier if all your devices are Apple. When you want to transfer the raw file from an Apple phone to an Apple computer, you just use the Airdrop function and it's there in seconds. If either or both of your devices aren't Apple, you need to physically plug your phone into your computer and wait for ages for the file to transfer. Apple's default editing software iMovie is also so much more user-friendly than equivalents on other providers. I do 90% of my editing using the right and left clicks of my mouse.

Whilst I tell people that they don't need to be spending thousands on tech to start filming videos, I will be honest in admitting that investing in Apple products has made my life far easier. When my dad died, I used some of the money he had left me to buy a MacBook and I already had an iPhone. I spent an hour in the Apple store at a video editing workshop. To this day I probably only use about 50-60% of the things I learned in that one hour to cover all my editing requirements. Six years later I have upgraded versions of those same devices to cover all my video needs.

Do you need to go out and spend thousands on Apple products to start filming videos? No. Do you need to learn video editing to start filming videos? No. I'd say you can get by for months and maybe even years without editing a single video. That said, editing is something that will at some point make your life easier and be something you want to bring into your video practice.

Probable Option: Tripod

If you are choosing to use your phone to film video, then you probably will need to get a tripod at some point. Unless you are doing exclusively social media shorts, or walk and talk videos, filming on your phone can be a pain (and it can also be a pain only being able to do shorts or walking videos). Trying to balance your phone on bookshelves and mantelpieces so you don't have to hold it doesn't work long-term. At some point in your filming, you are going to want that little upgrade.

To give you perspective, I bought my tripod about eight months into my video journey. I used my webcam and walk and talk up until that point. I bought a MANFROTTO Tripod (£60 / $80) and a MANFROTTO Phone Attachment (£30/$40) off Amazon. This served my filming requirements for a further FOUR years. No extra tech investment is required. If you are filming on phone, this is a value-for-money purchase that is going to save you a lot of hassle and give you the foundations for years of filming decent video.

Possible Option: Microphone

Whether you speak into your desktop or phone, they each pick up the sound clearly. In that sense, you can speak using the default microphone for the rest of your speaking career.

Nonetheless, there is a noticeable improvement when you use a microphone. It takes out that "tinny" sound that comes through when speaking on desktop in particular.

You are not a music producer or radio DJ, you do not need to invest thousands into a hyper-sensitive mic'd up studio. Two super cheap options give you a noticeable improvement to your audio.

Let's say that the audio quality of the default microphone is 5/10. Functional, yes. Beautiful, no.

I can get that audio quality up to a 7/10 for free. When editing a video in iMovie, I use a simple option called "Voice Enhance". You click it and it automatically adds a crispness to any vocal noise (i.e. not music or background noise). Another one of the reasons I recommend investing in a MacBook and using iMovie for your editing. Technically not "free" considering that initial investment, but after filming hundreds of videos over the past six years, I think that function has paid for itself by now.

Apple saves the day again when it comes to the next, inexpensive option. If you plug a set of Apple headphones into your desktop or phone, the microphone now sits close to your mouth thanks to the design of the headphones. This takes the sound quality up to about an 8/10. I use Apple headphones whenever I am sitting at my desk to speak, for example during meetings or workshops on Zoom. I even sometimes plug them into my phone for doing Facebook Lives. The limitation of the headphones is that being plugged in, they do require you to stay in the same position. You couldn't do an active, standing speech as you would yank them out and lose your audio. But for speaking from a seated position, or even doing a walk and talk holding your phone, they're great. These headphones cost about £20-30 ($35-50). That's a small investment to noticeably improve your audio quality.

To upgrade beyond this, you are starting to look towards three figures. To get the audio quality without compromising on movement, you will need a label mic like a Lavier, or a Bluetooth mic like a Rode. To get your audio quality up to about a 9/10 with a fixed microphone, the industry favourites are Blue Yeti and Rode microphones. You are looking at $100+ for these. These are nice but, to keep things in perspective, I still don't own any of these yet. They are nice to have but don't limit me from doing any of my key speaking activities.

Get your first couple of videos under your belt and then, if you haven't already, grab yourself some Apple headphones and that will tide you over for a long time before you need to consider your next upgrade.

Possible Option: Halo Light

You can get away without a halo light for a long time. When I first started whispering videos into my webcam in the early hours of the morning, a halo light would've been nice, but it wasn't the most important factor in my videos at that point. The fact that I was having to whisper and that I didn't have any experience speaking on camera affected the video quality far more than the dodgy lighting.

As I got a slightly kinder schedule, I would film videos whilst walking in good daylight or in rooms with plenty of natural light. In the summertime, this wasn't a problem. Living in Scotland, this was a bit harder in the winter but I could still film a video with okay lighting if I picked the right day and time.

I probably wouldn't have even bothered with my first halo light if it wasn't for a special set of circumstances.

In 2017 I went to a business expo. It was awful. The organisation was amateurish and the guest speakers were pretty dull. After a couple of hours, I decided to do one last loop of the stalls and then head home early.

One stall caught my eye "Ideas into Action". The branding looked more professional than the others I had seen and I was quickly accosted by a bouncy lady.

"Hello," she said, "what brings you to the expo today?".

As we got chatting, I found out her name was Karen and she was a business coach. Unlike many "business coaches" that I have met over the years, she actually had a personality and told me that she used to be in a rock band and that she had grown up next to the Cadburys Chocolate factory. She was like a female Willy Wonka.

"I've just started hosting business boot camps," she informed me, "and because I grew up next to the Cadbury's factory, I like to give out Golden Tickets to come along for free. I've got one left today, would you like it?"

Like Charlie Bucket, I eagerly accepted the last one and as I left that expo I felt that the day hadn't been a total waste of time after all.

I went along to that first boot camp and struck up a relationship with Karen and her wife Kate. I ended up getting coaching from Karen and through her network, I met tons of great people. I met a lady who ran a centre where I ended up hosting all my Edinburgh workshops. So many of Karen's community ended up buying my book when I ran my 2018 Author Your Life book tour. I met another coach who to this very day helps me promote the monthly virtual summits I host in the Rise and Inspire Facebook Group. I even met the photographer for my wedding thanks to Karen!

In 2019, Karen was diagnosed with cancer. I went to another of her boot camps in December and although she was bubbly as ever, I had a feeling this was the last time I was going to see her.

Karen died in February 2020, a week before my massive Valentine's Day breakdown. It's only after a period of reflection and lots of therapy that I realise that this might have been the event that unconsciously triggered everything for me. It was an echo of losing my dad five years earlier and made me consider if I was going the right way down the path I had set out on after Dad's death.

When Karen died, her wife Kate barely had time to organise the funeral and collect herself before COVID lockdown hit in March. After we emerged from that first lockdown in the summer of 2020, Kate started wondering what to do with Karen's stuff.

At their house, they had an outhouse that served as Karen's office. She had massive whiteboards, cameras, laptops, lights, you name it. Kate decided to sell all these items to the community and if I remember correctly all the money was donated to the hospice that had taken care of Karen. This is how I came into possession of Karen's halo light. There's also a really funny story of the journey I made to collect that halo light. It's on my YouTube channel called "The Monster in my Car". The halo light is well used; it tilts at a slight angle; it is perfectly imperfect. Even when I add new lights to the collection, I'm always keeping this one. It's a little memento I have of Karen and allows me to carry on her work in my own way.

Even when I came into possession of a halo light, I did not buy it in the traditional sense, and I would've probably been fine until that winter when another lockdown hit, and I was starting to rely on virtually speaking from home. All that is to say that you don't "need" a halo light until you are regularly speaking, and even then can wait a little longer if you don't live in a seasonal part of the world with dark winters.

Am I adding more to the current halo light I have now? Absolutely. But that is six years into my speaking career and two years into my virtual speaking career. All you need right now is a camera and an internet connection. You can add the extras gradually over time.

I.   You need a webcam or phone camera
II.   Video editing software will be of great aid
III. A tripod will improve your filming on phone
IV.   Microphones can amplify your voice
V.   Lighting can sharpen your image quality

Chapter 5

The Key Attributes Of A Virtual Speaker

Every revolution is made possible by the characters within the movement. It is their traits and strengths that drive things forward. The Virtual Speakers Revolution is no different. Certain qualities help speakers stand out in the virtual environment that is so often populated by monotonous robots armed with powerful, pointy weapons (yes I mean your HR department with their arsenal of slide decks). To beat the robots, we need to see your humanity. In this chapter, we'll explore some of the key ways you can show that.

Authenticity

Authenticity has almost become an oxymoron nowadays, it's used as a cliched buzzword that doesn't mean anything, or by assholes trying to justify themselves. Of all the words to suffer in this way, it's a bitter irony that using the word "authentic" no longer feels authentic.

But let's try and put those trappings aside and get back to the root of the word. In the virtual world, you have a much harder time earning people's attention. Therefore, you have to offer something different. The only thing that you can truly offer that is different is yourself.

A lot of workplaces aren't happy with personalities. They will want you to "tone it down" and "be professional" in your speaking. They want corporate robots who can be relied upon to do the safe thing the same way each time. I don't understand why businesses would give up their competitive advantage in this way. If the beginnings of this century have shown us anything, it's the rise of the personal brand. Founders are often as well known or even better known than their companies and celebrities have name recognition without people really knowing why they are famous.

We like personality. We don't always like EVERY personality, but we want to be offered the opportunity to make that judgement for ourselves.

In many of my speeches, I make Star Wars references and use analogies from Star Wars to help explain concepts. I even have a storytelling workshop based entirely around Star Wars. Do I do this to be trendy or tap into popular culture? No, I do it because I love Star Wars, and that's part of the package you buy into when you hire me as a coach or speaker. Don't like it? Then find someone different. Do like it? Then we're going to have a blast together.

I know that my passion for Star Wars may not be considered "professional" and it will repel some people. That's okay. I'm more worried about who it will attract. Who you attract with your speaking is far more important than who you repel. You will never be able to reach everyone with your work and message, so you need to clarify who you want to reach. You don't attract anyone by toning yourself down and playing it safe. You attract people by making it clear who you are and what you're about.

You have to let your personality shine through as a speaker. There is no "right" way to be a speaker. You don't have to mould yourself into some persona of what you think a speaker "should" be that doesn't feel right for you. Bring your passions and pastimes into your presentations. Show your audience who you really are. Some people won't be interested, that's okay. Some people will love you for it, and they're the ones who matter.

Vulnerability

If you thought being authentic sounds tricky, then wait until we dig into this next attribute. Being authentic might sound unrealistic or scary to you, but you can see the appeal of it, can't you? It would be nice to be more like yourself when you are speaking and showcase things that make you happy or excited.

But what endears people to you is not diamonds, but coal. They aren't interested in the glitz and glamour until they've seen the raw materials. They want to know your flaws before they appreciate your strengths.

In the online world, we are constantly shown snapshots of success and it gets a little boring. They might earn a "like" but we don't really like them. When someone starts a speech by telling you how good they are at all these different things, how interested are you in what they've got to say?

It's not that we can't be inspired by achievement or success, it's that we want to understand the journey. We want to see that someone has struggled because we struggled. We want to see someone who has failed because we failed. When we see that someone has struggled and failed but still succeeded, then it makes us feel that even though we might struggle and fail, we can still succeed too.

That means being vulnerable when you speak. Not the controlled vulnerability of talking about mistakes you are comfortable with ("It took me ages to park the car today, aren't I silly") or even worse the humble brag disguised as struggle ("My Harvard degree left me with a lot of student debt"). Real vulnerability exposes your flaws and doesn't paint you in a good light. It's talking about the times we were careless or thoughtless or heartless. It's admitting the times we were selfish or lazy or nasty. This is the dark side of being human that we all struggle with (Star Wars reference for you there).

One of my speaker friends talks about the time he didn't report a fault in a lorry he was driving because he couldn't be bothered filling in the paperwork. One of his colleagues drove that lorry and was involved in a crash that could've killed him. That's vulnerability.

Another of my speaker friends talks about her cocaine addiction and the time she came in from a party and left one of her bags of drugs lying around. Her daughter found one of the bags and almost ate some of the cocaine. That's vulnerability.

Neither of these stories paints my friends in a good light, do they? But I can assure you that they are lovely, kind, supportive people. I wouldn't be friends with them otherwise. I don't judge them on these mistakes they made, I judge them on what they learned from these mistakes and how they've become better people as a result. I can appreciate the people they are now more because of the mistakes they've made in the past and the work they've done to rectify them. We also can't pretend that there isn't a part of us that could've made the same mistakes that they did.

We need the vulnerability for true connection. And in an online world where connection already requires more work and we are shown the highlight reel constantly, vulnerability is what is required to bridge the gap and form connections across borders and oceans.

Creativity

If you have had to sit on back-to-back meetings and webinars, you know that things can get monotonous fast. Endless agenda points and slides do not hold your attention for long. In the online world, you have got to mix things up. We will cover specific techniques to consider later in the book, but for now, let's focus on the principle behind the techniques. You have got to be creative.

Don't be afraid to try new things in your virtual speeches. We moan about people reading PowerPoints to us, but then we don't do anything different when it comes time for us to present. If you try something that doesn't work, you don't have to keep doing it. But if you stumble upon something, that gives you a new edge that you didn't have before.

When lockdown first hit, I was sure that you should maintain a consistent distance from the camera. Then I saw one of my clients lean in to whisper to the camera and I realised I was wrong, playing with the distance could be used to good effect.

When I was on board with playing with the camera distance, I still maintained that the camera should remain stable and never be moved. Then I saw another client move the camera to different vantage points in her house, and I realised that moving the camera could work too.

I have tried things that didn't work (trying to use a physical flipchart whilst on Zoom was an experiment I won't repeat) but most of my experiments have paid off. They aren't things I would do all the time (shaking my cat's food bag at the camera requires some context) but I have them in my locker as tools that I can utilise when appropriate.

Allow your creativity to come through in your way. If you're musical, how could music come into your speeches? If you're artistic, how could drawing come into your speeches? If you feel that you have no such specialised talents, don't think you aren't creative. Creativity is not an attribute restricted to the arts. Creativity is just trying to bring new ideas into existence. We can all do that. Make sure you permit yourself to try that in all your speeches, virtual or otherwise.

Now that we have looked at some of the key attributes of a virtual speaker, let's look at some of the key practices of one.

I.   *You can't be anyone but yourself on camera*
II. *There is strength in showing weakness*
III. *Do things differently*

Chapter 6

Consistency Is Key

Confidence on camera will only ever come from one thing: consistency. You can read about all the tips and techniques in this book but ultimately that doesn't matter if you never go and put them into practice. You have to create a regular video schedule and in this chapter, we're going to cover an outline of the key factors to think of for creating your regular video output.

Frequency

Do you get fit, strong, and healthy if you go to the gym once a month? Of course not. Do you get fitter with a weekly workout? At least a little right? For me, nothing is consistent unless it is being done at least weekly.

How does this look for your virtual speaking? It means you should be filming at least one ten-minute video each week. It doesn't have to be fancy, just turning on the webcam or phone and speaking into it. This is all I did for months starting out in 2015.

You might ask, can I do smaller videos instead of one big long one? My answer is that you can do smaller videos in addition to one longer one, I think that's fantastic and will give you extra experience and confidence. But to return to an exercise analogy, running 26 one-mile runs is very different from running a marathon. In a smaller video, you have a smaller margin for error and will only speak about a topic on a shallow level. It doesn't give you a true representation of where your speaking is and it doesn't force to you grow and improve in the same way. A long video will expose your weak points and make obvious areas for improvement. You might get away with losing your place in a 2-minute video, it will stand out when you do it multiple times in 12 minutes. You will get away with not having gestures or facial expressions in a 50-second video. It will be painfully obvious when you watch yourself doing it for 15 minutes on camera.

If you want to take your virtual speaking seriously and want to get paid at some point for the speaking you do on camera, know that no one is ever going to pay you to speak for 60 seconds. They want to see a flowing speech with a tight structure, engaging storytelling, and empowering themes. You will simply never be able to develop those skills unless you speak in a long format. You don't have to be banging on for hours and hours, but don't fool yourself into thinking that filming a bunch of TikToks makes you a virtual speaker either.

A false barrier that a lot of beginner speakers put up is that they don't think they have time to film videos, probably because they think of videos in terms of scripts and post-production. We're not filming Hollywood movies here. We're not even filming cult B-movies. We're recording you speaking your thoughts aloud into a camera. We minimise the work before and after your video so it makes it feasible for you to build the weekly consistency of filming them.

In my previous book "Rise and Inspire" I talked about the importance of filming videos without a script. Training yourself to speak without relying on memorisation and/or following a word-for-word script. Turn on the camera and start speaking. When you make a mistake, speak through it, don't linger on it. When you lose your way, keep speaking until you get back on track. When you forget what you were going to say, just move on to speaking about something else. You can film a messy but complete video in this way, and you can always use editing to tidy up anything that was really incoherent. This means it won't take you all week to prepare for one ten-minute video and you don't have to do hours of post-production on it. Write down a few keywords about what you want to speak about, turn on the camera and just start speaking about them like you would if you were explaining them to someone over a cup of coffee.

How To Come Up With Speaking Topics

As you come to terms with thinking about filming weekly videos, the next thing you might be wondering is "how am I going to come up with something fresh to speak about each week?". This is very easy, especially in the beginning, because you haven't spoken about anything before! The world is your oyster. Of course, you do want to develop a specialism and expertise. You would probably find it odd for me to start randomly bringing speeches about nutrition, stocks, or artificial intelligence into my public speaking work (although I could speak about small areas of crossover, for example, how certain foods and drinks affect your voice). In the beginning, though, you are still finding and refining what your topic of expertise is (my topic of expertise when I first started speaking wasn't even public speaking of course). This gives you more freedom to explore where your passion and expertise lie. There are a couple of suggestions I have to tap into this.

Share something you learned that week

I used to build my first videos almost entirely on the books I was reading, the podcasts I listened to, and the videos I was watching. If something I had learned from one of these stood out to me, I'd shoot a video on what that was, why I found it interesting, and how I thought it could be applied. Rather than try and build your speaking career on the sand, build it on the solid rock of what's come before you. Whilst you shouldn't just become a mouthpiece for other people's wisdom (I see this too often in the self-help world), every speaker stands on the shoulders of giants. Did I make up everything I know about public speaking? Of course not, I learned it from people who were better than me at it. Can I provide my own slant on public speaking, absolutely. When I type "virtual speaking" into the books section of Amazon, (before publishing this book of course!) do you know how many titles with that keyword come up?

"Virtual Speaking": 0
"Speaking Virtually": 1
"Presenting Online": 1
"Virtual Speaker": 1
"Virtual Platform": 1
"Virtual Events": 2

I'd say I'm creating something fairly original here, but I'm not starting from scratch either. I'm building on what I've learned from years of public speaking and teaching people how to translate that into speaking online.

Share something that happened to you that week

As a speaker, you want to be building up a library of anecdotes, analogies, and metaphors that feed into your speaking topic. No one speaks on an original topic (even with virtual speaking, I predict that the list of books on Amazon will be much more substantial in a couple of years). What makes you stand out is the way you structure and present your material.

The stories you tell are such a key part of this, so practice them. Shoot a video talking about an event or experience from the week. Learn how to introduce key characters, describe scenes, and convey emotion. Share how that experience impacted you and what your audience can learn from it.

Recycle something you've previously spoken about

This might seem like cheating, but it's anything but. If you try to redo a video from 12+ months previously, you will not be able to make it look the same. You will have a greater range in your voice, your gestures will be more pronounced and your vocabulary more expansive. As you grow more confident in speaking, you will want to redo old videos. This isn't to say that you are ashamed of them or that they weren't useful to people at the time, you can just add more depth to them. Don't be afraid to return to old ideas from a fresh angle with your speaking.

Where To Post Your Videos

After you've filmed your video, it's time to decide where you are going to post it. Do you have to post your videos? No. Do you have to be a speaker? Also no. Speakers need audiences. If you aren't willing to put your work in front of an audience, I think you need to consider whether speaking is the right pursuit for you.

What freaks people out when they first consider filming videos is that they think thousands of people are going to be watching and judging their imperfect origins. That is nothing less than delusions of grandeur. You don't need to worry about being judged on your first videos, you need to be prepared for being ignored.

When you first start posting videos, a few of your close contacts will be mildly interested, they will watch one or two and then get back to their regular lives. You are going to be posting tumbleweed trailers for months and this is fantastic! It gives you time to build your craft whilst nobody is paying attention. After 6-12 months, maybe a little longer, of posting consistent videos (by consistent I mean at least once a week) someone is going to watch one of your videos and say "this is quite good actually". There's your first fan and you build from there.

When I'm talking about posting your videos, I'm not saying that so that other people can watch them. Very few will. The main reason is for your personal accountability. When your last YouTube video was three weeks ago, you'll notice. When you haven't posted a social media short on Instagram for ten days, you'll notice.

Additionally, you want to be building up a library of content. When someone is watching a video of yours that captures their interest (it will happen), they will go to watch more. If they see that you only have five videos, they are going to be discouraged and think that perhaps you aren't as much of an expert on the topic as they hoped. But if they see that you have dozens of videos, it not only serves them more, but it makes you look more credible too. When you go to my YouTube channel and see that my first video was posted in September 2015, and there are hundreds of videos after it, it makes you think that I perhaps know a little about speaking on camera, right? You want to make that same impression on your audience too.

What platforms do you want to post on? The decision-making process behind which social media platforms you want to be on is something I went into more detail on in my previous book "Rise and Inspire". The next Declarations will also cover the different virtual platforms in more detail, and that may inform your choice too.

For me, every speaker should have at least a YouTube channel. That is a specialised video platform and forms a "bank" of your videos if nothing else. It is easier to find your old videos when they are on your YouTube channel, than trying to scroll through hundreds of posts on a multi-purpose social media platform.

You probably want a place where you can post long-form videos apart from YouTube (long form in social media terms is technically anything over 60 seconds. But for me, long-form is at least 5 minutes). The major platforms that allow you to do this are Facebook, Twitter, and LinkedIn.

You may also choose to have a platform where you can post short videos. Instagram and TikTok are the platforms that specialise in short-form videos, although there is nothing to stop you from posting short videos on the same platforms you post your long videos. The reverse isn't always true however, Instagram and TikTok have time limits on the videos you can post, although you can post edited excerpts from your longer videos. Some content creators do this successfully by hosting their longer videos on YouTube and directing their audience to them with teaser trailers on Instagram/TikTok. Although you may find that too time-consuming when you are starting.

There are a variety of considerations to take into account when choosing your social media. The long-form video platforms tend to have an older demographic, the short-form video platforms tend to have a younger demographic, to list just one distinction. Purely in terms of filming the video, however, this is how I would suggest you think of your social media.

Essential: YouTube
Probable: Facebook/LinkedIn/Twitter
Possible: Instagram/TikTok

At the very least, you should be uploading your videos to a public YouTube channel, then sharing them on one social media platform. That is enough accountability in the beginning. That accountability will help you build consistency, which allows you to start developing all the techniques that we have talked about in this declaration.

I.   Mastery lies in little and often
II.   Material is all around you
III. Choose your key platforms

Chapter 7

How To Start A Video

One of the key challenges that people tell me stops them from filming videos is that they don't know how to start them. The first thing I tell them is don't worry about how to start them, just start them! Turn the camera on and start talking. Worrying about how to start a video is one of the many forms of procrastination that hold people back. You don't need to be perfect in the beginning, in fact, you won't even be good. Embrace the flaws and imperfections of starting out. It's something you will look back on in the future romantically.

Nonetheless, to build your virtual speaking skills, you will have to add some refinement at some point. There's a definite stage I notice in beginner to intermediate speakers. They are more comfortable speaking on camera, they just don't do it very well. A key mistake that I so often see is how they begin their speeches.

The key thing you've got to remember in virtual speaking is that people are not obliged to listen to you. If your Facebook Live isn't engaging, they will scroll past. If your YouTube video isn't doing it for them, they will click the next suggested video. If your Zoom workshop isn't interesting they will just log out. Even if you are running a meeting or delivering a presentation for your job and your colleagues have to attend, there is nothing to stop them from sitting on their phones or clearing out their inboxes rather than paying attention to what you're saying. In a physical setting, there is more social pressure for people to pay attention and not sit on their phones or walk out of the room. In a virtual setting, there are no such barriers.

You have no right to your audience's attention online, you have to earn it. This is why the start of any virtual speech is so crucial. You have to communicate quickly to your audience what's in it for them. Most speakers simply don't do this, and I'm not just talking about the beginners. There are two key mistakes I see in the way that virtual speeches are started.

The first is the "sweet nothings" approach. This is arbitrary small talk like "how's everyone doing", "nice to see you", and "thank you for joining today". Although I observe this behaviour across the English-speaking world, there is a definite "Britishness" to this. You're not hosting a tea party. You don't have to tick off items of etiquette. Honestly, the audience isn't interested in telling you how their week went, they want to know how you can help them. There is a time for interaction, but these types of formalities do nothing for creating that interaction.

The second approach is the "CV/Resume opener". This is where the person tells you all about themselves.

My name is David McCrae and I live in Scotland. As a virtual speaking coach, I help aspiring speakers find their voice, tell their story and share their message. I have a Master's Degree in Psychology and I have been a professional speaker for six years. I have published five books, three of which are #1 Amazon bestsellers. I have won five national public speaking championships and hosted a podcast with an audience in 50 countries around the world.

It's not that this information isn't relevant and you can't share all or some of it. From reading this book, you already know this information about me because I have shared it at appropriate points. But can you imagine if I had started with that? Boring! Here's an uncomfortable truth. Your audience doesn't care about you. Not in a nasty way, but they aren't watching your speech to find out more about you. They want to find out more about them. They don't care about you until they find out how you can help them. When they understand what you have to offer them, then they will warm to you more as a person.

If you are to avoid these two key mistakes, then how do you actually start a virtual speech? My answer differs slightly depending on what platform you are presenting that speech on, whether it is live or recorded, and whether you can interact with the audience or not. We will dive more into these nuances in the rest of the book. For the moment, there's a fairly generic template that I'll walk you through that will serve you reasonably well in most scenarios, and certainly be a whole lot better than the sweet nothing and CV approaches you may be relying on just now.

Hook

There is a bit of a myth that people online have an attention span shorter than a goldfish. There are mad single-figure estimations about how many seconds you have to earn someone's attention. In my experience, you can give your audience more credit than that. If someone has clicked on your video or signed up for your webinar, they aren't going to abandon it in 3-9 seconds. I'd say that you have more like 30-90 seconds to prove to them why it's worth their while to keep listening. After that time, they will assess everything they have heard up until that point and decide whether they are going to scroll on, click something else, or turn off their camera and open a new browser window.

This still means that every sentence counts, and right from your first sentence you need to be building evidence that you have something of value to say to them. This is why I encourage speakers to think of what their opening "hook" is. In fishing, 99% of the time is spent waiting for the fish to go for the bait, and only 1% of the pursuit is actually catching them. Similarly, 99% of your effort as a virtual speaker is trying to get people to watch your speeches in the first place. If they aren't "hooked", they aren't going to hear all the hard work you put into the rest of your speech.

Speaking hooks come in different forms, but the key principle behind all successful hooks is that you spark the audience's curiosity. As humans, we can't stand unanswered questions. Look at common trends in online clickbait articles: "12 things you didn't know about How I Met Your Mother (Number 8 will blow your mind)"; "Is this the best sporting comeback ever?"; "Why this walrus is winning the internet this summer". Each of them in their own way sparks a question (What is number 8? Is this a sport I like? What's special about walruses?). If you can form a question in the audience's mind right from the start of your speech, they are going to listen until they get a payoff, which is the second thing that each clickbait title promises (Your mind will be blown. You'll see an incredible comeback. You'll find out what's special about Walruses).

The most obvious way to create a question in the audience's mind is to ask one! You can ask rhetorical questions ("Who said that the only way to be productive was to sit in an office between the hours of nine and five?"), hypothetical questions ("If the internet collapsed, what would happen to humanity?"), open-ended questions ("In what ways can we build customer loyalty?") and personal questions ("Why did you start your business?). It's important that you actually answer the question in your speech. I know this seems obvious, but don't think you can use a provocative or controversial question to reel people in and then talk about something different. Remember I said that people don't like unanswered questions? If you leave them hanging or don't attempt to address the answer at all, they will associate the annoyance of unfulfilled curiosity with you, and don't count on them ever watching one of your videos again.

Another easy way to spark curiosity is, to begin with a story. The natural pattern of beginning-middle-end that stories follow means that the audience doesn't have their curiosity satisfied until the end of a story. You can start from the beginning of a story and work your way through it in a conventional sense. Alternatively, what I find particularly effective is to start a story in the middle to grab an audience's attention, give them the backstory of what's happened and then present the resolution.

Questions and stories are the "low hanging fruit" when it comes to starting a speech. There are two techniques that are a little more advanced but can be great alternatives to the question or story. The first is to make a promise. If you start your speech with a promise like "This company can triple its revenue this year"; "What I share with you today will help you film a fantastic video on a shoestring budget" or "Better sex: guaranteed" then the audience is either excited or skeptical enough to want to hear what you've got to say to back that up. Similar to the advice on questions, don't make a promise you can't fulfil. Your audience will never watch you again if they feel manipulated into watching your speech by an empty promise.

The final technique to spark curiosity at the start of your speech is an unconventional statement. This is a statement that sounds like it isn't true or dispels a common belief. Some of my favourite examples that I use in my speeches include "Half of all TED speakers are introverts"; "You do not have to sound professional to be an effective speaker" and "If you are trying not to feel nervous whilst speaking, you are wasting your time". One of the most powerful ways to spark curiosity in someone is to make them question something they believed was holding them back ("I'm an introvert so I can't be good at speaking", "I don't sound professional enough for anyone to pay me"; "my nerves stop me from speaking"). If you can get them to question that belief and suggest that there is an alternative for them, then they will listen to you with optimism and even excitement. That's about as "hooked" as you can ever get someone.

Relate

Sparking the audience's curiosity is important, but it's not the magic pill that's going to get them to stay. Think about traveling around your town. Is there a restaurant or bar where you look through the windows and think "that seems nice, I'll have to go there sometime". How many times do you travel past that establishment without ever acting on that curiosity? You probably still haven't been there have you?

Think about another similar venue that you used to travel past a lot, but now frequent on at least an occasional basis. What changed? I'm betting that it was more than just curiosity that made you walk through the doors one day. It was some kind of purpose: a family dinner, a friend's band played there, or a first date. You didn't act on that curiosity until you had a reason to act on that curiosity.

This is the next thing that you have to give your audience. You have to make it clear how your talk relates to them. You might have piqued their interest with your opening hook, but they aren't going to keep listening to your speech if they are only interested. You have to turn that interest into investment. You do this by bringing them into the speech.

The techniques that you use at this point can look similar to what you've done at the hook. Ask them more questions, bring them into the story you are telling, and make them a promise about what they are going to learn in your speech. The difference is that with the hook you are trying to attract their attention as quickly as possible, here you have more time. You can go into a little more detail and direct it more towards them as an individual. For example, if you have opened with the question "In what ways can we build customer loyalty?" you might follow that with "Think about a time when you had a fantastic customer experience. What made that so special for you?". If you had begun with the promise "This company can triple its revenue this year" you can then lead into "Think about all the tasks that you do in your working day that drain your time and have no meaningful impact on your daily output. How many hours per day do you think gets sucked away from you by menial activities?". If you had kicked off your speech with the unconventional statement: "Half of all TED speakers are introverts" you can then focus on the audience by saying "As an introvert, you choose your words carefully, you're a great listener and a deep thinker. All of these attributes allow you to connect with your audience in ways that an extrovert struggles to.". Can you see how each of those examples brings more focus onto the individual audience member and makes them engage more personally with your topic? (And I just did it to you right then!).

Curiosity brings your audience to the door, relatability makes them walk through it. Once they are inside the establishment, they are going to hang around and see if they like it. If you pull off these two steps successfully, then your audience is going to stick around and give your speech a chance.

Introduce

When you have earned your audience's attention by telling them what they can get from your speech, then you can tell them more about yourself. As I said earlier, it's not that the audience doesn't care about you in a nasty way, it's that they care much more about finding out about themselves first. Once you've done that, they will still have some curiosity left over to find out more about you.

This isn't to say that you launch into telling them your life story or working down a list of achievements, That is still a mistake. The experiences and achievements you share should still have some relevance to your audience. One of the most significant experiences in my life was my parents getting divorced when I was four. That has shaped my character and my life experience probably more than any other single event in my life. Do I tell my audiences about that when I'm speaking? No. One of my notable achievements is that my high school basketball team got to the national final. I have a runners-up medal from it. Do I tell my audiences about that when I'm speaking? No.

Neither of these relates to my topic of public speaking or my themes of expressing yourself and sharing your message. You have to share aspects of yourself that your audience can continue to relate to and thus see themselves in. Do I share the equally significant life experience of losing my dad to cancer? Yes. Do I share my other national trophies for winning speaking competitions? Yes. But I'm not sharing these just for the sake of them, I'm sharing them because they still involve my audience. The story about my dad makes the audience think about making sure they didn't end up on their deathbed with a message unshared. My competition trophies show that audience that in a couple of years you can go from sitting in your student flat waffling into your webcam to getting recognition on national stages.

Sharing more about yourself ultimately is what sets you apart from the other people in your industry who essentially speak on the same thing in probably a similar way. It's just about being strategic about what you share and when you share it. You have to ensure the audience's needs are served first and that you share information about yourself that still relates to their experience and journey.

If you follow this structure, you are going to have more people staying on your videos and getting benefits from all the life experiences and hard work that you have to share.

I. *Spark curiosity*
II. *Relate it to them*
III. *Show that they can relate to you*

It Is Declared!

Your Movement Matters

You probably won't be attempting anything on the scale of Biden's Presidential Campaign, but you are trying to reach new people in new ways. To do that successfully, there are certain foundations that you have to establish.

The first is to get your basic technology setup and, as you read, we are talking REALLY basic. The technology that you need to be a virtual speaker is already in your possession. You don't require a PhD. in computing to be able to speak online. You have what you need literally in your pocket. Revolutions begin with a single camera.

The second is to embrace the attributes of a successful virtual speaker. To show up authentically, connect with vulnerability, and harness your creativity.

Next, you have to establish a routine so that you can consistently work on your virtual speaking skills. This begins by ensuring you are frequently taking the opportunity to film video, any little opportunity, any time you can grab it. We established that you have a wealth of speaking topics to cover in these videos, from years of education to everyday anecdotes. Then we started the process of thinking about where to post these videos.

Finally, you want a process that will get you started every time you find yourself in front of a camera. First, you must hook your audience by sparking their curiosity to get their attention.

Second, you relate what you are going to say to your audience to demonstrate why you deserve their attention. Thirdly, you introduce yourself so that they can begin the process of connecting with you as a person.

In the following declarations, we are going to dive further into the techniques for filming these videos, and the platforms you can use to broadcast your message.

Declaration Two

Be Charismatic On Camera

The video showed two labradors eating out of their bowls. There's nothing remarkable about a greedy Labrador. Only slightly more remarkable was the Scottish voice narrating their feast. You had to be an avid follower of the niche sports of rugby, tennis, or golf to recognise the smooth tones of sports commentator Andrew Cotter. You might wonder why anyone would be bothering to film two dogs eating.

What was remarkable was the timing. Two weeks before the video was published, Cotter should have been commentating on the final weekend of the Six Nations, Europe's most prestigious rugby tournament. Instead, the final round of matches had been cancelled due to COVID and we were now one week into national lockdown. Cotter, in his lockdown boredom, had set up a "game" between his two pet labradors Olive and Mabel, and decided to commentate on that instead.

The video exploded on Twitter. It was shared by publications such as The Telegraph and The Guardian, picked up by broadcasting powerhouses such as CBS and ABC, and retweeted by celebrities ranging from Ryan Reynolds to Gary Lineker. It soon racked up 8M views across all platforms.[9]

---

[9] Cotter, A. (2020). *Olive, Mabel & Me.* Black and White Publishing. Edinburgh.

Requests poured in for more videos and sequels such as "Game of Bones" and "The Office Meeting" drew in millions more views, attention from publishing companies and celebrities, and even lead to Cotter getting a book deal to publish "Olive, Mabel and Me" later that year.

Cotter himself admits that the star talent was not him, but his two labradors. The dog is the ultimate performer on camera. They have no insecurities or performance anxiety, communicate so much emotion through their facial expressions and body language, and build fantastic rapport with their audience. There's a lot we speakers can learn from our canine companions.

This Declaration is centred around getting us as comfortable on camera as a dog. This is where we no longer think about being on camera and the camera is an extension of our natural expression. Several key principles will allow you to become charismatic on camera.

The first is a mindset shift around how you perceive the camera, seeing it as an ally rather than a foe. Next, you need to build the habit of actually looking in the camera! We'll explore what it means to have an "active window" and we will examine some more advanced skills that you can develop with the camera.

Chapter 8

Make Friends With The Camera

When the recording light shines and you see your face on the screen, what is your reaction?

For most people the types of words that come up are: "nervous", "awkward", "frozen", "self-conscious", "fidgety", or even "dread". These reactions are perfectly natural when you consider how most people see the camera: as an opponent to be wrestled with. My challenge to you is why do you think the camera is against you?

Consider for a moment how much that camera has helped you. It has helped you to stay safe in your home during a pandemic. It has enabled you to keep in touch with those you love. It may have allowed you to continue earning an income from the comfort of your own home.

Doesn't that sound more like a supportive friend than an opponent trying to trip you up? Really, the camera is the ultimate friend. It's always there for you and it never lies. The camera is always doing its best to please you but you're the one who keeps fracturing the relationship.

"Camera, you're making my face look weird," you protest one day.

"Camera, you're making me sound stupid," you reprimand the next day.

"Camera, you're making me feel nervous," you admonish another day.

Poor Camera just sits there and takes your abuse whilst continuing to be 100% honest with you.

The reason that the relationship is fractured is because you keep treating the camera like it's the HAL 9000 from 2001: A Space Odyssey and that it's somehow out to harm you.

If you want this relationship to improve, you've got to start bringing something else to the table. You can't keep projecting your insecurities and hang-ups onto the camera, because that is what the camera will show to your audience.

I understand that speaking on camera is something that doesn't feel natural and you haven't been trained to do it. The same was once true for riding a bike or driving a car though, wasn't it? But when you set your mind to it and persevered through the stages of feeling awkward, it eventually became effortless for you. The same will be true for you about speaking on camera.

The first step is to recognise that the camera is your friend and ally. It is not trying to hurt your feelings or trip you up. It wants you to succeed. It wants to help transmit your voice to different cities and different countries. In this virtual speaking journey, it will be your constant companion, as loyal as the dogs we were talking about earlier. If you develop a good relationship with it, you're going to have a lot of fun together.

Think of the feelings that come up for you when you know an old friend is coming to town, when you are going home for Christmas, or when you are being lavished with attention at your birthday party. Are you thinking of feelings along the lines of "excitement", "anticipation", "fun", "appreciation", "joy", or "love"? Imagine if these were also coming up when you speak in front of the camera? Excitement to start sharing a message you are passionate about. The fun of playing around with your audience. The appreciation of your audience thanking you for your help. These feelings are what you will start to experience when you stop viewing the camera as an opponent to be confronted but instead as a friend helping you communicate with the world.

Keep Your Eyes On The Prize

Where do most people look when speaking online? Take a moment to think. Was your answer....the screen?

Most people look at the screen because there is something there to look at. They are reading their slides that they are screen sharing, they are looking at people's faces in the Zoom boxes, or they are even looking at their own face on a selfie screen.

There is a good reason why most people do this. The human brain is wired to be attracted to faces. Even newborn babies demonstrate a preference to look at human faces than any other form of visual stimulus.[10] That's why our eyes drift towards the screen. There's one problem with this.

Your audience isn't on the other side of the screen. They are on the other side of the camera.

If you ever watch a recording of yourself speaking on your phone or desktop, you will realise very quickly that when you look at the screen, it looks like you aren't addressing the viewer directly. Your eyes will appear downcast if you are speaking on a

[10] Johnson, M. H., Dziurawiec, S., Ellis, H. D. & Morton, J. (1991). Newborns' preferential tracking of face-like stimuli and its subsequent decline. *Cognition* 40, 1-19.

desktop or a phone filmed in vertical orientation. Alternatively, it will appear that you are looking off to the side if you are filming using a phone in horizontal orientation.

Have you ever had a conversation with someone who just couldn't look you in the eye? They gazed over your shoulder or stared down at your feet. After even a minute of speaking to that person, how does it feel? Super awkward, right? It feels like there is a barrier between you and you just want to grab them by the shoulders and shake them as you plead, "Look at me!".

That is the effect that many speakers are having when they are speaking virtually. By looking at various distractions on the screen, they are inadvertently raising a social barrier between them and the audience. You instead have to raise your eyes to look through the camera.

This will feel weird because you will feel like you are not looking at the audience, as you may see their faces bobbing around on the screen below you. You also get no visual feedback when you look through the lens. On the screen, slides will be whizzing by and faces will be dancing through different emotions. However, that lens will never blink. It won't look right to you, but it does look right to your audience. When you look directly into the camera lens, that is when your audience will feel that you are making eye contact with them. You will appear confident and composed and you will also be able to build rapport and connection with them because you will remove that awkward social barrier.

Of course, I know what you're thinking now. Sure I get why I'm supposed to look into the camera, but how can I make myself do it? It is a habit you will have to build like anything else, but there are three tricks, the three Ps of good eye contact, that you can use to speed up the process.

Plane

One of the mistakes people make with their camera is that they don't have it at eye level. Usually, the laptop rests on a desk halfway up their torso or they cradle their phone in a hand that is resting well below their face. Firstly, let's talk about the odd dynamic this creates.

When you look down into the camera, it makes the audience feel you are looking down on them. It creates the impression that you consider yourself superior to them. It's like they are a little child being told off by a teacher or a parent. It creates resistance in them to what you are saying.

Less often, I see the reverse. Someone's desktop is so high on their desk, or they are extending a selfie stick above their head, and it means they are looking up into the camera. This creates the reverse impression, that you are now the little child saying "please listen to what I have to say". It robs you of your authority and expertise as a speaker.

The Goldilocks solution is, of course, to have your camera directly in front of your eye line. This creates the dynamic of speaking to your audience on a level playing field, meeting them respectfully rather than appearing superior or inferior to them. Not only does it remove any weird power dynamics, but it also makes it easier for you to look at the camera. When the camera is directly in front of your eyes, your gaze will naturally drift onto it more often, without you even trying. It's creating a default of automatically looking into the camera more.

Getting the camera up there will require a little innovation. Let me first state something that isn't apparent through writing. I'm 188cm (6ft4) tall. It takes a fair bit of effort for me to get a camera up to my eye level, but I've found a way. If I can, you can too.

For my laptop, I bought a laptop stand. Unfortunately, the laptop stand barely got the webcam any higher. So, I took the box that the stand came in and placed that on my desk. Next, I positioned the laptop stand on top of the box, then I put my laptop on top of the stand. That gets the camera up to my eye line. As an unexpected side effect, it also relieved a lot of neck and shoulder tension I didn't realise I'd been giving myself over the years by hunching over a laptop!

For filming on my phone, I use a tripod. Even when I have the tripod legs as narrow as they can without the whole thing falling over, it still doesn't come up to my eye line. My adjustment in this instance is to simply take a couple of steps back, and this creates the impression that you are being spoken to by someone slightly taller than you (which would probably be the case if we met in real life), rather than having some monster looming over you.

Invest in whatever apparatus you need to ensure you get that camera up to your eye line. It's a one-time intervention that will permanently improve the quality of your speaking.

Position

The next step seems relatively simple. You want to know exactly where your camera is. Like most simple things, people underestimate how easy it is to get it wrong.

When your camera is recording, whether on desktop or phone, a light normally comes on to tell you that you're recording. Fantastic. Except the light is a distraction. The light is not your camera. Unfortunately, when people start to find out they should be looking at the camera, they start looking at the light shining next to the camera. Whilst this is certainly better than looking way off camera at the screen, it still produces a mismatched image to the audience that you are almost but not quite looking at them. Of course, you will think you've fixed the issue and be none the wiser until you watch a recording of yourself speaking in this way.

Therefore, you want to know exactly where your camera is ahead of time. Find it at the top of your computer or phone when it is not recording and notice where the light is. When you are recording you can use the light to navigate, knowing the webcam is close to it, but you look into the lens and not the light.

Prompt

With the camera directly in front of you, it will become a little easier to look into it more often. However, your eyes will still be tempted back down to the screen or to go for a wander around your home office.

Firstly, let me just stress that the aim is not to have 100% eye contact with the camera. In regular conversation, we usually only make eye contact with someone about 60% of the time[11] and although in speaking we should be aiming for stronger eye contact, we don't want to develop the psychopathic stare either. Our eyes naturally move upwards or to the sides when we are

---

[11] Argyle, M., and Dean, J. (1965). Eye-Contact, Distance and Affiliation. *Sociometry*. 28: 239-304.

remembering, imagining, or planning. It's okay for these natural movements to occur when you are speaking, but we want to make sure that the eyes are moving from firm contact for these moments, rather than moving after already having bounced all over the place.

To develop a strong gaze into the camera, we can set up a prompt to help us out. This is a reminder that is going to constantly direct your gaze towards the camera. This can be as simple as a Post-it note with an arrow drawn on it saying LOOK HERE. Over lockdown, I've seen some imaginative attachments that people are placing on their cameras to make them more obvious. My favourite was a plastic smiley face that you attach to the top of your computer. The smile was cut out and this went over the camera, that way you look "into" the smile when you look at the camera. As well as being fun, this also quite neatly uses our brain's bias towards faces to work with creating the habit, rather than against it.

If you employ these three tricks, then you should start to develop the habit of looking into the camera more often and your audience will begin to feel the difference as you talk to them.

I.   The camera is your partner
II. Connect through the eyes
III. Remember the three Ps

Chapter 9

Have An Active Window

What do I mean by "have an active window"? Does that mean a pane of glass running on its little legs?

Of course not. In virtual speaking terms, the "window" is everything your camera sees. This window is normally a squarish box if using your desktop camera for something like Zoom; a long horizontal rectangle if you are filming with your phone in landscape mode (this is how I do my YouTube videos for example); or it could be a long vertical rectangle if you are filming with your phone in Selfie mode, to do a Facebook Live for example.

Everything in this window your audience can see, everything outside the window, they cannot see. Having an active window means making sure that what your audience can see through the camera is as engaging as possible. Speaking virtually removes some key body language cues. There's the long-standing joke that we never know if someone is wearing anything on their bottom half on Zoom. We, therefore, have to maximise the body language cues that we do have on camera. Fortunately, some pretty key ones are still very much in play for us as virtual speakers.

Face

One of the most important signals of emotion is our face. If you spend a short period in conversation with someone with a deadpan expression, you'll quickly realise how disconcerting it is when someone doesn't show much emotion on their face. Sadly, that's how most people speak on camera.

It's like Rigour Mortis has set in watching some people online. You can't tell whether the video is lagging or their face really does look that soulless. It usually needs a cat to jump on the keyboard or a child to tug on a sleeve to break down their robotic visage.

I understand that a lot of this comes from a fear of being on camera or difficulty feeling a connection with others through the digital medium. Equally, we are responsible for how we show up in life, and I'm sure if we were speaking to an attractive celebrity on Zoom we would probably be able to crack a smile fairly easily.

Quite simply, we need to allow ourselves to show more emotion when speaking online. The easiest way to do this is just to smile more. Smiles are infectious. We like smiling. Other people like smiles. Neuroscience shows us that when we smile, we feel happier as a result.[12] A lot of online meetings would be less painful if people smiled a little more.

Beyond smiling, allow the full spectrum of emotion to come through your face. When you are telling a story with a twist, raise your eyebrows in surprise. When you tell an amusing anecdote of a snafu you made, puff up your cheeks in exaggerated

---

[12] Ekman, P., Davidson, R. J., and W. V. Friesen (1990). The Duchenne Smile: Emotional Expression and Brain Physiology II. *Journal of Personality and Social Psychology.* 58: 342-53.

exasperation. As you share a disappointing outcome, let the corners of your mouth drop in sadness.

When I'm running workshops, a question I get asked a lot is how we can show emotion whilst still staying professional. I then ask the question of when it became unprofessional to be emotional? Should Martin Luther King have lowered his tone so that "I Have a Dream" was more professional? Should Stephen Hawking have stopped cracking jokes in his lectures so that he was more professional? Should Jacinda Ardern not have cried when citizens of her nation were murdered by a terrorist because that's "unprofessional"? We have millions of people around the world attending therapy because they aren't able to express their emotions properly. Our lives suffer from not showing enough emotion, our speaking is no different.

Hands

The partner-in-power to our face when it comes to virtual speaking is our hands. They are our second most prominent and important non-verbal cue after our facial expressions.

That's because our hands have evolved to be a sign of trust. In our caveman days, the way we would determine if another human was dangerous was to look at their hands. This was to check if they had a weapon in their grasp. If we could see their hands were empty, then we could trust them. [13]

However, if their hand was behind their back, then we didn't know what they might be concealing in their grasp. As humans grew more sophisticated and we developed clothes, we

---

[13] Van Edwards, V. (2016). *Captivate: The Science of Succeeding With People.* St Ives: Penguin Random House.

then started to shake each other's hands; this allowed us to use our other hand to check that the other person wasn't hiding a dagger up their sleeve. The modern adaptions of high fives and fist bumps all serve the same function of extending our hands towards another human to show that we're not a threat.

Although we no longer live in the Palaeolithic era, we still have the same brain from that period. Our brains have barely evolved in the last two million years and we still have a lot of our historic survival wiring built in. It might seem stupid to your most recently developed prefrontal cortex — the "rational" part of your brain — to be checking someone's hands for weapons, but your ancient brain is still running its survival protocols deep in your subconscious. So understand and respect what is going on in the caveman part of your audience's brain. One of the first things you want to do when you are speaking to an audience is to show them your hands. In particular, the "open palm" is a non-threatening gesture as the audience's Freddy Flintstone can "inspect" your hands. There are a couple of gestures I find useful for this purpose. The first is the simple wave "hello". The second is the "giving of gifts", you extend both hands towards your audience like you are holding an invisible present.

Our hands are more than just "trust markers" though. They are also a powerful extension of all emotional expression. This was demonstrated in a study of TED speakers. All people who are invited onto a TED stage are experts in their field with a message worth listening to, but some TED talks and speakers are much more popular than others. One of the key distinctions between the two turns out to be the way they use their hands.

The least popular TED speakers use an average of 272 hand gestures in their eighteen-minute presentations: while the most popular use an average of 465 gestures – nearly twice as many.[14] If you look at a speaker like Simon Sinek, who I consider to be a particularly accomplished speaker, he used over 600 hand gestures in his hugely successful TED talk "Start With Why: How Great Leaders Inspire Action".

Gestures therefore not only help us to build trust but also portray us as being more competent and confident. In virtual speaking, you have to make a concentrated effort to ensure the gestures you make are being captured by the camera. One of the phenomena I often observe is what I call the "Duck Under Water" gesturing.

Ducks are one of my favourite animals. They cruise along the water's surface, quacking away. It's an idyllic life. However, if you look below the water, you will see their feet are pumping rapidly. This is a good analogy for great speakers in general, calm on the surface, churning below the surface, but it is especially true for how amateur speakers use their gestures on camera. They often keep gestures at waist height, bouncing across the desk when sitting or locked in the gunslinger's position whilst standing. These gestures sit below the bottom edge of the camera window and the only sign your audience sees of them is an occasional jerk of the shoulder. As cute as ducks are, we've got to avoid imitating them online. When you are speaking make a concentrated effort to raise those gestures out of the water and ensure they are captured on the camera.

One question that I sometimes field in regards to gestures is whether they are too distracting. Firstly, people wildly overestimate how many gestures they are actually making. Remember that the most successful TED speakers used an

[14] Van Edwards, V. (2016). *Captivate: The Science of Succeeding With People*. St Ives: Penguin Random House.

average of 465 gestures in their 18-minute talks. That's 25 per minute or just less than one every two seconds. Most people who are worried about their gestures being distracting simply aren't anywhere near that level of frequency.

Secondly, I'm not advocating gestures for the sake of it. Flailing your arms around on screen does not constitute effective communication. Gestures should feel natural: extending your hand towards the audience when you ask a question; showing three fingers when you move onto your third point; making a chopping motion when you reach a decisive statement. These are all examples of congruent gestures i.e. the audience feels that the verbal and non-verbal communication matches. Can you imagine if I was talking about two ideas but held up four fingers? Or I'm talking about an achievement I'm proud of but I'm not smiling. That would also create incongruence between what the audience is hearing and what they are seeing. We gesture all the time in everyday conversation. These gestures are a natural expression of how we are talking at that time. Speaking is about learning to amplify those gestures that you are already using and allowing new gestures to develop that match and emphasise what you are saying.

Props

The third way we can make our speaking windows more active is through the use of props. As animated as we wish to be on camera using our face and hands, virtual speaking can still sometimes be a case of choosing between watching a talking head and reading a slide deck. Props are a great way to add visual stimulation beyond human features but also capture meaning better than words can.

A prop is just any object that you show to the camera and as such is it hard to define what props to use and how you should use them. Rather it's easier to give examples of when props might be appropriate.

A. Starting your speech: you can bring an object onto camera, perhaps a mysterious or ambiguous object, and start revealing small or partial details about what it is or why it's significant. That will spark curiosity in your audience and draw them into your speech.

B. Telling a story: stories by their nature are highly visual. Your audience will imagine scenes as you describe them. A way to clarify key visual aspects for them is to show them important items from that story.

C. Anchor a key idea: If there is a message that you want to drum into your audience, again and again, you can of course repeat it to them verbally. But sometimes a more effective method is to have an object that they immediately associate with the idea, and will remember every time you show them that prop throughout a speech.

D. Explain a difficult topic: ideas that are highly conceptual or academic might be a little tricky for your audience to follow. Sometimes a prop will get the message across clearer than lots of words, stats, and figures.

E. Comedic effect: a prop can be a great "reveal" for the punchline of a joke. Sometimes you don't need to say anything at all, but just show the object for the audience to start hooting.

What About Virtual Backgrounds?

Quite often when I am talking about active windows, someone will ask me the question about virtual backgrounds. I smile and inform them that I have a bit of a vendetta against virtual backgrounds.

Since the pandemic started, I've observed a bit of an obsession with virtual backgrounds and filters, and we've seen some funny viral examples of people turning themselves into potatoes and cats during work meetings. I can perhaps understand the reasoning behind them before the pandemic. If you were making a call from an open plan office and there was a lot of hustle and bustle behind you, maybe you wanted to hide that with a calming background of a Japanese water garden. Equally, if you were needing to work from home and didn't have a proper home office, you perhaps wanted to create a bit more of a professional environment with a backdrop of the New York skyline.

Lockdown, however, broke down the pretences we were trying to portray online. Everyone had to work from home and most people weren't set up for that. We saw people working off dining room tables and tucked away in bedrooms. We saw the washing hanging up, the kids' toys strewn over the floor, the junk that we hide away in the spare room and none of us gave a shit. We were all in the same boat and within a few weeks, we normalised the fact that people work from home in less than perfect conditions. We saw the humanity of people who had to juggle work and life. That was the type of authenticity and genuineness that we always claim we want to see in people but are reticent to show ourselves. Pre-2020 you might have been embarrassed to join a work call with everyone sitting in a fancy boardroom whilst you hid away in the bedroom that needs a new lick of paint. In 2020 you saw that the CEO could also do with renovating their house.

This brings me back to virtual backgrounds, there is not the same pressure to hide and put up a pretence as there was before. I take advantage of the fact that people can see behind me to showcase aspects of my personality. They can see my Star Wars memorabilia and my hiking maps. I put in a bit of cheeky branding by putting some of my books on display (perhaps you'll see this one on a Zoom window one day!). These provide great icebreaker opportunities that I would never have if people just saw a fuzzy image of the Golden Gate Bridge behind me.

This brings me to my real gripe about virtual backgrounds. Most people are not set up to properly display a virtual background. Unless you have a green screen or a blank wall, they simply won't stick. You'll have seen people with fuzzy backgrounds lean back in their seats and suddenly disappear. Or they hold their hand up but appear to be decapitated at the wrist. This is awful for speaking. How much of this chapter have I spent emphasising how important non-verbal communication is when virtual speaking? Why would you use something that impairs this vital component of your non-verbal communication? How can you show emotion on your face when it disappears into pixels? How can you use gestures when every second gesture gets chopped off? How can a prop be effective if it is obscured by a fuzzy image? You're damaging your speaking ability for what? Because you're embarrassed by where you live? Because you thought your audience would prefer a stock image that they're bored of seeing on every call? Or you thought that sticking your brand across your silhouette would be great marketing for you?

Anyone without a green screen should never use virtual backgrounds. They have no upside to them. If you do have a proper green screen, I have seen some creative uses of virtual backgrounds, with sudden switches of background for comedic effect or adding more immersion to a story. The examples I have seen were used by international public speaking champions. Unless you are at that level of speaking ability and have the proper technology, avoid virtual backgrounds.

If you work on creating an active window with engaging facial expressions, animated gestures, and even a prop or two, the audience isn't going to feel that your speaking background isn't interesting enough.

I.   *Smiles win hearts*
II.   *Hands build trust*
III. *Props hold meaning*
IV.   *Don't fade into the background*

Chapter 10

Changing The Shape Of Your Speaking Window

After covering the basic principles of effective speaking on camera, it's time to start dipping into the nuances and technical considerations. These are the finer points of virtual speaking that you can start to think about and incorporate as your speaking progresses.

The first of these considerations is thinking about the shape of your speaking window. You might think that this is a fixed entity you have no control over. If this is the case you're half right. If you speak using the camera on your desktop, for example on a Zoom call, the shape of your camera will always be the same, a slight rectangle that is a little longer horizontally than it is vertically. This will always be the window you are working with and you can make the most of that, for example setting up your desired background (not virtual!) to appear when you are on calls or using your webcam to film something. This will also be true if you are using a professional camera setup, although I suspect this doesn't apply to many readers.

The other choice of camera is the phone, and here you can change the shape of your speaking window quite dramatically. Depending on whether your phone is filming vertically (think taking a selfie) or horizontally (think getting a family photo at

Christmas) you have different options and different advantages (plus a few drawbacks too). In this chapter I'm going to outline the choice between the two and when you might want to lean toward filming vertically, and when you might want to lean toward filming horizontally.

Advantages Of Vertical

Virtual speaking largely exists because of the selfie. The ability to just hold up your phone, speak into it, and share that message with the world is what has made the Virtual Speakers Revolution possible. We have become familiar with the vertical angle of our camera for pictures and videos. The strength of the vertical camera is the feeling of intimacy it creates. As you hold the phone close to your face, your audience feels like they are directly opposite you in conversation. This advantage is amplified by the fact that most social media platforms are designed with a preference for phone, rather than desktop. It means that when someone is watching on their phone, your video can blow up to fill their entire screen, making it feel like they are the only person you are speaking to. This bestows some key advantages to filming your videos vertically.

Walk And Talk

In 2016, there was a massive shift in virtual speaking. Two key developments happened on Facebook and Instagram. On Facebook, they brought in the live video feature. On Instagram, they upped their video limit from 15 seconds to 60, transforming it from a photo-sharing app to a credible video platform. This was a game changer for "casual" videos. It meant that if you had an idea that you thought was worth sharing, you could just take your phone out of your pocket and either broadcast it live on Facebook or sum it up in a short Instagram video (which you could then crosspost to Facebook anyway).

At the time I embraced these changes to start shooting regular "walk and talk" videos. At that time I didn't have a car so I did a lot of walking and figured that listening to podcasts wasn't the only way to make this time productive. I started recording little "Instagram shorts", 60-second videos that I posted on Instagram and then crossposted to Facebook. I started with daily videos and then found a more optimal number for creativity and engagement was 3x a week. After doing hundreds of these videos, I can tell you one thing...

It is much easier to hold the phone vertically than horizontally as you walk, especially when they reversed the trend of making smartphones smaller to making them bigger. Trying to hold the phone horizontally is like trying to hold a small TV one-handed. You often can't see the screen properly because your hand or wrist is in the way and so you can't see comments if you are live, or even just generally orient where you are on the camera. These "walk and talk" style videos are a great way to fit videos into your natural routine and they also add that element of authenticity that audiences want to see. If you are going to incorporate them into your speaking, then use the vertical angle to save yourself the hassle.

Easier To Look At The Camera

In a previous chapter, we talked about how people tend to look at themselves on the screen, rather than look at the camera. If this is something that you are still doing a lot and trying to work on, then filming vertically can help mitigate the effects if not looking into the camera.

If you film horizontally, it is really obvious when you are looking at the screen and not the camera. You look to the side of the camera and it creates the impression that you are constantly speaking over someone's shoulder. When you speak on a desktop, the distance from the centre of the screen (where people are usually looking when speaking) to the camera is much larger than on the phone, so again the discrepancy in the angle between where you should be looking and where you are looking is more obvious.

On the other hand, filming vertically on the phone reduces these discrepancies. It lines up the camera with your face on the screen, so you don't have the obvious askance gaze of horizontal filming. Equally, the distance between the camera and the centre of the screen on a phone is far smaller than desktop, so the angle between where you should be looking and where you are looking is smaller. For this reason, vertical filming can be a great option whilst you are working on improving your eye contact with the camera. Of course, this is not a licence to stop working on improving your eye contact, just because there is a way around it. Your vertical filming will still be better if you are speaking into the camera, and vertical filming does have limitations which means you can't use it all the time. Before we talk about those, let's cover the main advantage of using a vertical camera angle.

Live Interaction

The real advantage of the vertical camera is apparent when you are shooting live video. One of the most important aspects of live video is interaction with your audience. We will go into much more depth with this later in the book, but for now, know that the comments feature is one of the key components of live interaction. When you are live, comments will scroll up from the bottom of the screen to about halfway up. This is halfway up your screen regardless of which way you are filming.

When you are filming vertically, this means the comments go halfway up the long side of the phone. This often allows three or four comments to be visible on the screen while you are filming. But when you film horizontally, the comments are going halfway up the short side of your phone. I don't think I've managed to see more than one comment at a time when going live with my phone horizontally. Going live with your phone vertically, therefore, conveys a massive advantage for being able to track and respond to comments, especially when they are flying in thick and fast.

Advantages Of Horizontal

Although we've highlighted the strengths of vertical, I would still say that it's usually the inferior option to horizontal. When I'm filming a video, I only use a vertical camera perhaps 20% of the time now, even though I used to film more often with a vertical camera in the past. I will cover a couple of the minor considerations first before I get to the decisive factor that makes me choose Horizontal most often.

Viewing On Desktop

Desktop is designed for horizontal viewing, not vertical. This means that when you upload vertical videos, live or prerecorded, onto a desktop, you get these black "tramlines" on either side of it. It makes the video look smaller and also somewhat amateurish, even if you're filming in high quality.

It's important to remember that although vertical filming can be viewed fine on mobile, it doesn't translate as well to desktop. Horizontal filming, on the other hand, can be viewed equally well on both.

Stability

When you are filming on your phone, it usually means you are just holding it in your hand. This is fine for a 60-second short but if you are filming for even a few minutes longer, your hand and arm start to get tired and you need to switch the phone to your other hand and arm. A couple of minutes there and you need to switch again. This isn't too big a deal, but it can be a nuisance and it makes vertical filming less tenable for long-form video.

You can get tripods and stands that will hold your phone for you in the vertical position. My tripod has an adjustable attachment that allows you to place the phone either horizontally or vertically. However, if you are settling down in one place for an extended period of filming, I'm starting to wonder if vertical filming is worth it for you because of the next two factors.

Background And Props

When you film vertical, you are pretty much just a talking head. This makes it difficult for the camera to pick anything else up. If you want to show your audience something in the background, for example, a diagram you've drawn on a whiteboard, you often have to move to the edge of the camera or off it entirely for them to see.

A similar problem arises for props. The prop often obscures your face when you show it to the camera, which affects the quality of your voice and hides key non-verbal cues in your face.

A solution to this is to have the phone mounted on a tripod rather than in your hand, and stand further back from the camera; that stops you from being a talking head. But the further away you are, the less you will be able to read live interaction, which is the key benefit of being vertical in the first place.

The next factor is an even trickier limitation.

Vertical Restricts Gestures

Remember the last chapter I was banging on about how important it is for you to amplify your gestures when speaking virtually? This vital component of virtual speaking is almost wiped out by vertical filming. You can squeeze in a waggling hand around your shoulder and chin area and that's about it. Even if you mount the phone and stand further back, your gestures still end up tucked close to your body. And when you are standing further back, it reduces or eliminates your ability to interact with live comments. If you're standing too far away to read the comments, then you might as well be filming horizontally and give yourself the extra space. This is the key reason why I opt for horizontal filming the vast majority of the time, as gestures are simply too important to sacrifice.

Vertical vs Horizontal Comparison

The balance of the argument for me weighs much more to opt for the horizontal angle when filming. It is more versatile and more practicable most of the time. That being said, there are a couple of key scenarios that I think do favour the vertical angle.

1. A short to medium live video (5-15 minutes) that you want to be very interactive.
2. A prerecorded short video that you are going to post to a mobile dominant platform like Instagram or TikTok
3. A live or prerecorded video whilst walking

In these scenarios, I would say the vertical angle has an edge over the horizontal angle. Most of the time though I would recommend investing in a tripod and setting yourself up for horizontal filming.

Front Camera Or Back?

The final consideration after working out the orientation of your phone is whether to use the front camera (taking a selfie) or the back camera (taking a family photo). At the start of my filming journey, I was doing my walk and talks into the selfie camera, but for my YouTube videos, I was putting the phone on a tripod and filming into the back camera. At that time, there was a difference in quality between the front and back camera and so you wanted to use the back camera whenever you could to improve the video quality. When live video gained traction, you of course didn't want to speak into the back camera, as then you couldn't see the screen to interact.

I suspect this is a key reason why the front cameras on phones have now vastly improved in quality. The back cameras have their fancy assortment of lenses and zoom to take brilliant photographs, but the front cameras are shooting HD video now.

For this reason, I never use the back camera for filming! Live video is always into the front camera, even for my prerecorded videos like YouTube, I find it useful to see myself on the screen and track where my gestures are and ensure that they are staying in the speaking window. The same is true for tracking if my audience can see any props I bring onto the screen or things that I might be writing on a whiteboard behind me.

I know that people sometimes find it a bit distracting seeing themselves on screen but that's just the way live video is and I think you have to not only get used to it but see it as an advantage.

Now that we've covered which angle the camera is at, it's time to start thinking about how far we are from that camera lens.

I.   *Go vertical to move and interact*
II. *Go horizontal to be stable and expansive*

Chapter 11

Move In Your Speaking Window

When speakers first start speaking on camera, they often look like a stunned stone statue: their face fixed in a centuries-long stare and feet cemented to the floor. In the last few chapters we've hopefully given your face some animation, now it's time to spread that further down the body.

When the COVID-19 lockdown first hit, I remember that I used to tell people to stay a comfortable distance from the camera. Too close was creepy, too far was aloof. Once you found the Goldilocks point, you just stayed there until the end of the video.

I soon realised my error when I saw speakers breaking this rule successfully. One of my clients in particular made a habit of coming close to the camera to smile and whisper and I realised that I had to change the way I was teaching people about their distancing from the camera. Movement is far more important to virtual speaking than I first thought.

Default Position

Let's begin where I was partially right (got to protect my ego after all). There is an optimal position where you want to stand from the camera most of the time. In this position you want the camera to see your face clearly to pick up the facial expressions and allow you to perform expansive gestures without them shooting off the sides of the speaking window. You also want to be close enough to read live comments on the screen. I find this distance is between 1 and 2 metres, depending on your camera angle and height. Your head and shoulders should be in the top half of the speaking window and some of your torso in the bottom half (don't feel that you have to present from the waist up, especially if you are lanky like I am, that often means standing too far back).

You want to ensure that your speaking space is clear enough for you to comfortably step forward to the camera (e.g. don't have your tripod resting on the far end of a table) and comfortably step back as well (don't speak with your back against a wall). I appreciate such extravagant space isn't always possible speaking from the comfort of your own home, so if space is limited you can speak against the wall but ensure you've got space in front of you to step into. The effect of coming nearer to the camera is only really created by you actually coming close to the camera, not just moving from further across the room to a point slightly closer. The effect of moving away from the camera is created just by moving away from the camera, regardless of how close you are to begin with. So you can move from close to the camera back to your default position, as well as move from your default position further back in the room. Ideally, you have the three points, close, default, and far, but you can still pull off the techniques outlined in this chapter by moving between close and default. Let's start examining those techniques in more detail.

Near

The first time I noticed my rule being broken successfully was when my client, Jenn, was coming closer to the camera to whisper. It created the effect like it was just the two of us having a conversation and she was trusting me with a secret. I realised that what she was doing was a powerful rapport builder and it made me think of how else this dynamic could be utilised in virtual speaking.

The main aspect to understand about coming closer to the camera is it creates a sense of intimacy. Intimacy is "into me you see" and your audience can feel that when you are staring down the barrel of the camera you can see right through them. For the audience to feel safe rather than exposed in this scenario, you want to come closer to the camera to build trust with them. How Jenn did this so well was by whispering little secrets to the camera like "I know you don't shower every day" or "It's okay to still not have a clue what to do with your life". It gives the audience license to admit their flaws and feel safe in your presence. When they feel that, it changes the dynamic of approaching the camera from one that could be perceived as threatening to one that feels supportive.

I've noticed a particularly effective way to do this is through humour. I remember after Jenn had whispered "I know you don't shower every day" she followed that with a "Guess what?" and a pause..."I don't shower every day either". Coming closer to the camera creates the impression of an "in-joke": that Jenn and the single person watching (in this case me) were the only people who were cool enough not to shower every day, whilst every other moron is wasting their time getting wet every 24 hours. Coming closer to the camera makes your audience feel like they are in on the joke and that creates a bond between the two of you like you are "the cool kids" at school. By the way, I don't shower every day either. That's why I love virtual speaking.

The second important effect of coming closer to the camera is that it has an immersive effect. It pulls your audience into what you are saying. This can be effective when telling stories. I remember a literal example of this when another one of my clients, also called David, was telling a story about visiting his sister at Christmas. He told us how he got to the door of his sister's apartment and as he knocked on the door, he reached out to the camera and rapped on it. This was effective as it made us feel like we were his sister on the other side of the door, creating the impression that we were looking through the lens of the camera in the same way that his sister would be looking through the spy hole of her apartment door. We didn't just feel we were listening to the story, we were a character in the story. What sets apart master storytellers is their ability to bring us into the story in this way.

This technique works beyond just this specific example though. Coming closer to the camera, in general, draws us in and can be utilised to build dramatic suspense. Imagine that I telling the short story below, and with each sentence, I'm getting a little bit closer to the camera.

"The rain was pouring down as I hurried along the pavement. I darted between two parked cars and poked my head out of my hood to look one way, seeing nothing. I rushed past the

cars and looked the other way but a screech filled my ears. My head snapped around and there was a car hurtling towards me, the headlights blinding me and horn deafening me. It was going to hit me. "

As I tell that story, my voice would get faster and louder and I would lean into the camera, creating this bubble of tension. The audience is hanging on those words, wondering what's going to happen next.

There's a final consideration when thinking of distance from the camera, and that is when you are describing travel. This could be literal distance. Imagine you were telling a story about approaching a casket at a funeral. As you take one step closer in the story, you take one step closer to the camera. We can also think of travel as "time travel". In Western culture, at least, we talk about going "back in time" or "looking forward" to the future. Therefore when talking about the future, optimism, and aspiration, stepping closer to the camera aligns with our language, and stepping backwards will help an audience "time travel" to the past, as we will cover more in the next segment.

Far

To a certain extent, we can see moving away from the camera as the "opposite" of moving closer. If you want the reverse effect of moving closer to the camera, then step further back. There are of course nuances to this, so in this section, I'm going to show the "other side" of what we talked about in the previous section point by point.

We talked about one of the key advantages of coming closer to the camera being a sense of intimacy. So does stepping away from the camera mean that you are "not intimate"? Not exactly. Remember that intimacy without trust is just intrusiveness, so coming close to the camera in an inappropriate manner or before you've earned your audience's trust is actually going to repel them rather than attract them.

It would be more accurate to say that standing further from the camera is "disarming". It alleviates an audience's fears that they might have about you or what you're saying. If I was delivering a workshop about confidence and nerves in public speaking, it might sound something like this:

"It can be intimidating watching professional speakers who just seem so slick and smooth. They never flub a line, never break a sweat, and when they tell a joke the audience is roaring with laughter. You look at these speakers and think you could never look that natural."

What are the audience's fears here? There are several, but the root fear is that there is something fundamentally different between them and successful speakers. They don't have the "secret speaking gift". How do you get to that root fear? Here's what I would say next.

"You might even be thinking right now, it's all right for David. He's someone that this comes naturally to as well. (Step back) This is not the case. If you put a stethoscope to my chest right now you would hear my heart thundering. If you stuck a

drip in my arm you would detect elevated levels of cortisol and adrenaline. No speaker ever overcomes their nerves, the pros just learn how to channel them. In fact, the nerves are necessary for optimal performance. Speakers need the burst of adrenaline just like the Olympic Athlete needs it to give us the edge."

That step back at the key moment takes me off a pedestal a little. That small retreat disarms the audience. Rather than step forward to try and force confidence on them, I step back to expose my nerves. At that point, the audience will resist me telling them that they can be confident, but they will be attracted by me revealing I feel the same as them. If you try to approach your audience too quickly, metaphorically as well as literally, their shields will be up. If you disarm them first, then they will be open to welcome what you have to share with them.

A particularly effective way to achieve this can be through self-deprecating humour. Stepping back at the same time you make a joke at your expense is a one-two punch that thoroughly knocks you off that pedestal. Nonetheless, I do warn beginner speakers away from self-deprecating humour, as they often end up being self-deprecating but forgetting the humour ("Sorry this live is rubbish, hahaha") but if you are good at not taking yourself too seriously and are a more advanced speaker, this is a fantastic way to build rapport with your audience.

In a similar vein, stepping back can also relieve any dramatic tension that you have been building in a story. Do you remember my example from earlier about being in a rush on that rainy day and crossing the road but stepping right in front of a car? Here's how that anecdote ends.

"...My head snapped around and there was a car hurtling towards me, the headlights blinding me and horn deafening me. It was going to hit me."

"I dived back in between the parked cars and it missed me by a whisker (Step back). I received some furious beeps of the horn as the driver resumed their journey. I was soaked from landing in the gutter but had avoided the worse fate."

I would release the tension in that story in several ways. After building my voice to a loud fast crescendo, I would drop it down to a more regular tone. A look of relief would come onto my face. And I would step right back from the camera to reduce my intensity with the audience. Coming further back from the camera is one of a constellation of cues that signals to the audience that the tension is being released and they can relax again.

The final consideration for moving away from the camera is to signal travel, either through distance or time. Imagine telling a story about encountering a protective dog, and as you talk about backing away from it, you step back from the camera. Similarly, if you are telling a story where you go "back in time" then you can again stand back from the camera.

You can also stand back from the camera to give you more scope for sideways movement. One of the key limitations of virtual speaking is that it limits your ability to move side to side unless you have someone behind the camera who can track your movements or a fancy camera that can do so. The further you are from the camera, the more you can move whilst still being in the speaking window, so if you want to get particularly animated whilst telling a story, for example, then stepping back can give you a little more room to do so.

Near vs Far Comparison

The table below summarises how changing your distance from the camera influences aspects of your speaking.

Speaking Factor	Near	Far
Connection	Intimacy	Disarming
Humour	In-Joke	Self Deprecating
Storytelling	Build Immersion	Release Tension
Travel	Closer	Further
Time	Future	Past

Don't get too flat-footed when speaking on camera. Whilst staying in your speaking window restricts movement, it doesn't eliminate it completely. The dynamic of being on camera actually gives you opportunities that you wouldn't have with a physical audience. How would my client David have been able to create that "spy hole" effect speaking on a physical stage? Virtual Speaking is not just a substitute for physical speaking, it is a genuine alternative that allows you to do things that you wouldn't be able to pull off with an in-person audience. The back-and-forth fun you can have with the camera is one of those factors.

I.   Balance being intimate and disarming
II. Use different types of humour
III. Engage with storytelling
IV. Move in distance and time

It Is Declared!

The Camera Calls

Through this second declaration, you have learned the key principles of the most important foundation as a virtual speaker: being confident on camera. Whatever communication and technology developments are to come, you will need this skill.

You've started to make friends with your partner and ally in virtual speaking: the camera. You're breaking the bad habit of not looking into the camera and learning to make what your audience sees more engaging with your facial expression and gestures.

On top of these basic foundations, you can build more advanced skills by thinking of how you play with your camera angles and change your distance from the lens.

This is just the beginning. As you start to develop confidence on camera, you will realise that you have to apply more nuance. The camera doesn't lie, but it adapts depending on what platform it is transmitting through. You will have to learn the key differences in how your speaking changes depending on what platform you are speaking on. You'll learn more about this in the next three declarations of the Virtual Speakers Revolution.

Declaration Three

Thrive On Live

"Good morning everyone", the cheerful face fills most of the screen. Behind her, we can see out the rear window of a car and hear the low thrum of the engine. "I've got news that I want to share from the back of the car and unfortunately I didn't have any other time to do this."

You probably wouldn't expect a country's national leader to announce their first rollout of the COVID-19 vaccine in this way, but that's exactly what the Prime Minister of New Zealand, Jacinda Ardern did.[15]

This was by no means unusual for Ardern. This was one of many Facebook Lives that she has used during the pandemic to supplement and even, in this case, substitute for traditional means of communication. Moreover, she employs many of the important skills of successful communication on Facebook Live.

She speaks with a smile and shares personal information. In this particular announcement, she shares with the audience that she is speaking in the car after a three-day trip across the country because that is preferable to trying to do a live when she gets home and tries to put her two-and-a-half-year-old to bed. It's this warm authenticity that helps her build rapport with her audience.

---

[15] Watch the announcement here: https://www.facebook.com/jacindaardern/videos/247332813558373. Retrieved 17th January 2022

She also makes an effort to engage with her audience. When she has wrapped up her key information, she takes the time to address questions in the live chat, calling out the names of participants such as "Craig" and "Helen" as she does so. This is the type of direct democracy that the ancient philosophers of Athens could only dream of.

Ardern has combined traditional media with social media in a manner that the Washington Post described as a "masterclass in crisis communication".[16] Near the peak of the crisis in May 2020, 59.5% of New Zealand rated her as their "preferred prime minister", the highest score ever polled for a New Zealand Prime Minister.[17] It was no surprise to me that Arden's Labour party secured a historic majority in the 2020 election, the first time a party in New Zealand has held a majority since introducing proportional voting in 1996. My home country of Scotland uses the same system and it is actively designed to prevent majorities. I can assure you how hard it is to "break the system"; it has only happened once here too in Scotland since our Parliament was formed in 1999. You have to be very popular to pull it off.

There are numerous reasons why Ardern and her party have developed that popularity, but with my virtual speaking googles on, I see the way that Arden has used social media playing a big part in it.

I was observing Arden go live on Facebook from the earliest days of the pandemic and I think she was the first world leader to really grasp the power of this medium. For decades world leaders

---

[16] Fifield, A. (2020). "New Zealand isn't just flattening the curve. It's squashing it". *The Washington Post*. Retrieved 24 April 2022.

[17] Pandey, S. (2020). "Ardern becomes New Zealand's most popular PM in a century – poll". *Reuters*.

used the most modern invention, television, to communicate with their nations. Think of the pre-recorded address from UK Prime Minister Boris Johnson that I opened this book with. Or the historic example we also covered of US President George W. Bush addressing the nation from the White House on 9/11. But that modern invention has its limitations. As you watch your leader read off the teleprompter, there is a sense of being "talked to" not "talked with". As they host press conferences, there's the feeling that you didn't get invited to the cool kid's party. It doesn't have enough intimacy and relatability.

Virtual speaking, however, is different. When Ardern speaks into her phone whilst sitting in her car, you feel like you are sitting in the car with her. As she shares information and anecdotes from her day, you feel like you are in conversation with her. As she calls out your name during the broadcast, you feel seen, heard, and understood. You simply can't do that through the medium of television.

If it's good enough for the most popular leader in New Zealand's history, I think it's good enough for us too.

Facebook Live is just one of several virtual speaking platforms that are available to you. Each platform holds its own nuances and requires you to add slightly different skills to the foundational skills we covered in Declaration Two. In this declaration, we are going to focus on the first platform: live video.

The main challenge with these live videos is that you are fighting for attention. We are going to look at how to capture and earn that attention to get people watching your live stream to begin with. Then you'll learn some of the techniques to keep them engaged and interactive with you during your stream.

The Revolution continues!

Chapter 12

Live Foundations

Carrying on from Jacinda Ardern's example, we're going to first examine going live on social media. Facebook is both the pioneer and I would say still the leader in live functions. That said, the other major platforms: Instagram, YouTube, LinkedIn, and TikTok are catching up fast. In this chapter, I will use Facebook Live as the reference point for what we are discussing, but the principles apply equally to other live functions, the user interface and functions of each live will just differ slightly.

Add A Description

Thinking about your live video begins before you even press record. One of the beginner mistakes I see frequently is people going live without adding a description to their video. Consider your audience for a second. If they see a video floating around on their social feed with no description, what incentivises them to stop what they are doing and tune in to watch it? Social media is full of decisions about where to put their attention, if you don't add a description to your live, you are providing them with a decision they don't have to make. They can rely on a default response of "don't watch".

You have to earn their attention for them to even click on your video, just like you have to earn their attention when they actually start watching it. You have to make that description more compelling for them.

If you think of the structure we talked about for starting a video, a lot of those same principles apply to how you word your description. The description is a shorter version of this, and there are two things I think you should focus on.

(1) Spark Curiosity: ask a question, tease a story, make a non-intuitive statement, etc.

(2) Promise a Payoff: tell your audience what they can expect to learn/change/improve after listening to your live

All your description needs to do is hit those two points. People aren't going to read a long description. They are going to make a quick judgement based on a small amount of information. You aren't trying to throw them a lavish dinner party with your description, you are just trying to get them to come in the door.

If you are finding that no one is watching your lives, I find the most obvious reason is that you aren't providing a description. Start adding this in and you'll notice your viewing figures go up.

Live vs Replay

Although live video allows your audience to be with you at the same time you are speaking, most of the time they won't be! No matter how much you promote a live and incentivise live attendance, most of your audience simply isn't going to join it live. That's because they know that can catch up with it on replay. The replay is a double-edged sword in this respect, on one hand, it ensures that you don't "waste" a live by doing a broadcast that no one joins. On the other hand, the fact that your broadcast isn't captured in a single moment of time does give people an easier decision to not join live.

Would I prefer lives to be consigned to a single moment in time though? Probably not. It is better to embrace the fact that you need to train your live skills to appeal to a live audience AND a future viewer. I'm sure there are official statistics out there somewhere, but in my anecdotal experience, I'd estimate that 90% of your views on a live come from a replay audience rather than a live audience. 10% is still a big number that you need to learn how to interact with whilst you are live, but you can't interact in such a way that would exclude the 90% who will watch in the future.

For example, if you do a live that requires you to build on feedback you are getting from your audience, what happens if no one is on your live? It falls flat. You can't rely on real-time interaction the way that you could in a physical setting where the people are there with you in the room at that exact time.

Equally, although this is much less common, if you do have people who on with you live and interacting with you, you can't just spend a live having a conversation with them. When someone tunes in on replay, they will feel that they are just watching a party they weren't invited to.

You have to interact with your audience in a way that:
(A) It doesn't matter if you don't get a response

(B) Means you can acknowledge someone if you do get a live response

(C) Allows a replay viewer to still interact even though you are no longer there physically

This might seem like some kind of Philosophy 101 problem "Is it possible to speak to someone and not speak to them, and be present and absent at the same time?". It's honestly not as hard as that! It just requires knowing how a few key techniques work on live. It's these techniques that we will delve into in the following chapters.

I. Describe what your audience can expect

II. Cater to both types of audience

Chapter 13

Simple Interaction

Let's start examining how we solve the philosophical problem of interacting with a live audience and a future viewer at the same time. Before we start to outline techniques, I want to highlight one phenomenon you need to be aware of "engagement hacks".

Since social media was invented, people have been trying to find ways to play the system. In the early years of Instagram, you could put 30 hashtags on your post, meaning that people would be drawn to you through lots of different searches. After a few hours, you could then edit the post to delete the hashtags and then add them again. This would return your post to the top of the timeline on those hashtags, allowing you to "milk the cow" multiple times. On Facebook, you could boost your page on people's news feeds by creating artificial engagement. You'd ask an obvious question such as "who thinks they are capable of being more productive in their life" and ask people to comment "yes" or "me" if they agreed. At the time the Facebook algorithm was weighted towards the number of comments, if something was getting lots of comments, regardless of how meaningful these comments were, it would get bumped up people's news feeds. At the time of writing, people have discovered how to do this on LinkedIn. They post a provocative poll such as "Do you think vaccines should be mandatory" and know that the number of votes and angry comments that result will bump their post.

Big Tech is not stupid. These algorithms adapt very quickly. Instagram changed the way hashtags work; Facebook changed how comments are weighted; LinkedIn will discriminate between stimulating and antagonistic polls. Clickbait tactics such as these have a short day in the sun. It is much better to spend your time learning the long-term principles of engagement than hoping you can keep finding the next gimmick.

I mention this because there are gimmicks on Facebook Live. One that has taken a surprising time to die off is #live and #replay. This gimmick involves someone doing a live asking the viewer "If you are watching live, put #live in the comments. If you are watching on replay put #replay". This comes from the outdated thinking that Facebook boosted posts in the algorithm based on the number of comments, not the quality of comments. When you are using this gimmick, or the inevitable gimmicks that come in the future, you aren't trying to interact with your audience, you are just trying to mine them as a data point.

Nothing is going to turn your audience off faster than thinking they are being treated as a data point rather than a person. There are ways to generate that interaction, engagement, and, yes, a resulting boost in the algorithm, that are just as simple but much more personal.

Using Names

One of the easiest ways of acknowledging live viewers is to call them out by name. When you are live, you will see the names of people who join live in the comments thread e.g. "David McCrae is watching live". The app changes all the time, and at the time of writing, it only shows the names of your Facebook friends who are joining live, which is a little annoying as when you speak as a brand most of your audience aren't your friends! I hope Facebook changes this, but I can understand that for larger lives having a stream of names joining could be a little overwhelming. Live will always show you the number of viewers with an eye and number in the top left-hand corner, so you can always acknowledge the viewers as they come in and ask them to leave a comment so that you can see who they are.

Whilst acknowledging your viewers by name or presence is a way of building connection, I see most speakers get a little too eager about this when doing their lives. They will blurt out someone's name as soon as they see it, usually interrupting themselves mid-sentence. Remember I said that most of your viewers are watching on replay? Think about what their viewer experience is like when you are constantly interrupting yourself to say hello to names and viewers as soon as they join. It's not a coherent speech and your replay viewers are more likely to disengage because of this. Remember that your replay audience are the vast majority of your total viewership, you are disrupting the experience of the 90% for the sake of the 10%. It doesn't make sense, does it?

There's an unfounded fear that if we don't immediately acknowledge our live viewers, we are going to lose them. Give your audience a little more credit. If they have been attracted by your description, they are going to stick around for a while and hear what you have to say. They will appreciate being acknowledged, but they aren't expecting you to roll out the red carpet for them as soon as they join the broadcast.

You should use natural pauses in your flow to take the time to acknowledge people. Finish your point, or at least finish your sentence, before you say hello. Even then, I find this form of acknowledgement a little arbitrary. You're saying hello just because that's what you're "supposed to do" on live. I think we can be more advanced in the way we connect with people.

When I see someone join live, I try to weave their name into what I'm talking about. For example, "A lot of speakers on Facebook Live feel pressure to say hello to everyone who joins in, is that a pressure you feel Jane?" or "You can give your audience more credit than that. This is something that we've spoken about before John, isn't it?" or "I see Chris has just joined, and she's a fantastic example for my next point". This means that you don't break your stride whilst speaking, your audience naturally slots into what you were going to say anyway. This way, you can get the benefits of live engagement without changing the quality of the viewing. If anything, it will make the replay audience feel that they missed out on the personal rapport you developed with your live audience and be more eager to join live next time.

Asking Questions

The low-hanging fruit of live is asking questions. Not engagement hacking questions, but genuine questions. Questions that allow you to relate more to your audience and also help them relate more to the subject of your live. There are some examples of generic questions that I see people using with good intentions, but they don't hit the mark.

"How are you today?" (*This question is rhetorical in real life, never mind on video*)

"What's the weather like where you are?" (*Only British people find the weather vaguely interesting*)

"What did you have for breakfast today?" (*And this will be relevant because...?*)

"Are you an author/coach/consultant/speaker who wants to earn more money" (*Nah I've always been fond of earning less money*)

Let's try again, shall we? When you are going on live, you need to think of personalised questions that relate to the topic of your live. That question I slated about what you ate for breakfast would be relevant if you were going to do a live on energy and blood sugar and were going to make some recommendations for good foods to eat for breakfast. I've just never seen that question used in a speech remotely related to nutrition.

There are some guidelines for asking good questions. First, we need to care about the answer. When you ask how the weather is where someone is, you don't really care, do you? It doesn't change what you're going to say whether the person is experiencing a heatwave or hurricane or anything in between.

Second, you want to be genuinely finding out information, rather than just getting someone to agree with you. This is the type of manipulative affirmative questions I see in pyramid schemes, sleazy sales, and disingenuous self-help. The "do you want to earn more money" is a classic example of this. You aren't interested in the audience, you just want them to agree with you, buy into what you do, and (probably) buy from you.

Third, the question needs to be useful to your live, but not necessary for it. At 20 seconds into your live, don't ask your one live viewer "Would you like me to talk about strength training or cardio training today?". They are probably just browsing and won't want to take on the responsibility of guiding your entire live.

How do we avoid these pitfalls? Firstly, we need to care about the answers. We do this by making the questions a little more personal to our audience. For my audience, I might ask "how long have you been a speaker?". From the answers, I can gauge whether the audience I'm addressing at that time is beginner, intermediate or advanced. I care about the answer because I'm going to pitch the level of my content differently depending on where I feel most of my audience is at.

Secondly, we want to be genuinely finding out information. Ask about scenarios that we know they are likely to experience. If I'm doing a live about speech structure, I'd ask "Do you have lots of ideas about what you want to say but no idea how to structure them?". If I get "yes" coming back at me in the comments, I can focus that live on how to pick key ideas. If I'm not getting yeses coming back at me, I might follow up with another question. "Do you find that you know what you want to say, but struggle to keep to the time allotted?". If the yeses start coming in for that, then I know that timing of content will be a better place to focus on.

Thirdly, make sure the question is useful but not essential to your live. To carry on from the previous example, I might not be getting much back from those questions I'm asking about structure. If I'm relying on those questions dictating what I'm going to talk about, then I'm floundering. Instead, I have already planned to do a live video about structure, and I've already planned content based on the questions I'm asking. I'm still going to cover that content, but if lots of people are telling me they struggle with keeping to time with their speech, I'm going to go into more detail on that particular part of my live to serve the needs that they've shared with me.

What makes questions so versatile is that they don't lose their effectiveness with a replay audience. They can still put their answers in the comments and get that feeling of "back and forth" with you even though it's not happening in real-time. Admittedly, the guiding aspect of questions does get lost on replay. If you find out that a ton of replay viewers were struggling in one area, you can't go back and make the live more relevant to that need, but that just gives you an idea of what you can cover in your next live doesn't it!

Get Creative

Questions are the standard way of interacting on live, but not the only way. There are lots of inventive ways to get an audience to interact with you. One of the speakers in my Facebook group, Carol Boston, says at key points of her live "that's a writer downer". At that point she's calling for the audience to interact with her live by writing down a key soundbite she's just shared. I've seen speakers hold an unusual object to the screen and ask the audience to write in the comments what they guess it might be. I've seen lives used for guided meditations. There are lots of simple ways that you can create that feeling of interaction with your audience, even when they are not watching you live.

With interaction, we want as many people live with you as possible, as that improves the quality of the interactions. In the next chapter, we're going to look at how to increase that live attendance.

I.   Don't rely on fleeting hacks
II. Call names
III. Question often
IV. Try new things

Chapter 14

Increasing Live Attendance

The most obvious reason (although not the only reason, we'll talk about that more later) why you want to go live is to have an audience there with you who you can interact with. You can't call out names, ask questions and do fun interactive activities if you have no one live with you! There are a couple of choices to make with live that determine whether you will get more live viewers or more replay viewers.

Scheduled vs Unscheduled

People are more likely to join you live if you get them a date and time to join you. The most successful lives in my Facebook group are not from me! They are from the speakers who speak at our monthly virtual summit "Inspire Week". Part of the reason why their speeches are successful is that they book a set time slot to go live, and they can promote that slot in the group so interested people can tune in live.

If you go live unscheduled, that means that people have to decide whether to interrupt what they are doing to watch you. If they are scrolling aimlessly, perhaps they will tune in. But if they have even a vague purpose for being on that social media platform, they are more likely just to stick with their current activity by default.

It might surprise you to learn, therefore, that I hardly ever schedule a live. Why? I think that scheduling every live takes away some of the attraction to the live. If someone sees you scheduling a live, they think it must be something special for you to put it in the diary that way. If you schedule every live you do, then how do you highlight a particularly important or interactive live? It's much harder now.

The more significant reason, however, why I hardly ever schedule a live is because it takes away the authentic, unpolished nature of a live. If you have scheduled a live, people think you have put a lot of preparation and practice into it and they won't see it as being something off the cuff and in the moment. Unscheduled lives create the impression of spontaneity. There is likely to be some prep and forethought into such a live, but it doesn't seem that way. For me, the feeling of having an authentic, real-time interaction with someone is the most important feature of a live. If you schedule every or most of your lives, you lose that key feature.

Scheduled lives have their place and help boost live attendance, but their effectiveness is through using them sparingly. Keep most of your lives unscheduled to maintain that feeling of spontaneous, authentic interaction in the moment with your audience.

Short vs Long

The second consideration that plays a big part in live attendance is the length of your live. This is fairly simple, the longer you stay live, the more opportunity you are giving people to see it and join. You'll quite often have the experience of getting to the final couple of minutes of your live and seeing a little flurry of people join in and start saying in the comments "Aw, I was enjoying that" or "Gutted I missed this, I'm going to watch the replay". This more often happens with shorter lives in say the 6-12 minute range. If someone joins 7 minutes into an 8-minute live, they've essentially missed it. However, the same 7 minutes into a 15-minute live means they have a chance to get their bearing, catch the gist of what you're talking about, and still enjoy half of the remaining value of the live.

Does that mean that you should go live for as long as possible to maximise live attendance? Similar to scheduled vs unscheduled, it's not that simple.

The first consideration to think about is when your audience thinks they've missed too much of your live to bother with the remaining portion. If they see you've been talking about something for twenty minutes, do you think they'll see much point in joining for what might be the last five minutes?

The second consideration is your replay viewers. Remember that they constitute about 90% of your total views. Consider this scenario. One of your fans, not a random eyeball on the internet but someone who supports and benefits from your work, sees that over the last couple of days, they've missed two live videos from you. One was 6 minutes long, the other was 26. Which one are they more likely to watch?

Of course, it's the shorter one. They might catch up whilst they are having lunch, taking public transport, or sitting on the toilet (don't pretend you don't do this!). A 26-minute video requires carving out a much more intentional period of time that sometimes people don't have, or don't want to create.

The fairly solid heuristic, therefore, is that the longer your live video is, the more likely you are to get live viewers but the less likely you are to get replay viewers. Shorter videos, on the other hand, are more likely to get replay viewers but less likely to get live viewers. I would define a "short live" as 5-10 minutes (any shorter and you're not giving anyone a chance to join you live at all) and a "long live" as 15-20 minutes (if you go much longer than 20 minutes, that's probably when you should think about scheduling it to ensure a meaningful live experience for your audience). The "Goldilocks zone" is 10-15 minutes. This provides the opportunity for some live viewers to join you and is appealing to a replay viewer also.

If you want to increase your live attendance, then a longer, scheduled live is more effective. Use such lives sparingly and strategically so they don't lose their impact. The shorter, unscheduled lives are your bread and butter, as they maximise those replay views that form the majority of your total views.

I.   Schedule for more live viewers
II.   Use short videos to attract replay viewers
III. Serve live viewers with longer content
IV. Find the Goldilocks zone

Chapter 15

Live Mistakes

After covering good practice for Live, it's prudent to cover some of the not-so-good practice. As is often the case, bad habits are more prevalent than good habits. Cutting out the bad habits is often a simpler and faster outcome to a better result than developing the good habits. In this chapter, you'll learn a couple of simple fixes for your live videos.

Waiting For People To Join

If there was a cardinal sin for live, I would say this is it. I know why people do this, and it makes sense in theory. The most important part of going live is having a live audience, right? Otherwise why not just post a prerecorded video? The issue is that a live audience is about more than just numbers, it is about the experience.

The way this scenario usually plays out is the speaker hits record. They sit barren-faced in front of the camera for 10, 15, 20 seconds. Next, they mumble "Just waiting for people to come live". They stare out the window, fidget, look back at the screen and see they have a live viewer. "HI JULIE," they screech, "WE"RE GOING TO START SOON" and then their emotion and animation disappear as soon as it arrives. Julie gets bored with the human elevator music and clicks on a cat video instead. Our speaker is a minute, sometimes two into their live and they have done absolutely nothing. How many live viewers has their waiting earned them?

Zero.

When you go to a concert, you don't go to look at an empty stage, you go to listen to a performance. On live video, you have to give your live viewers a performance from the moment they step in. The paradox is that if you wait for live viewers, you will not entice them to stay when they do arrive.

Furthermore, remember the key fact that 90% of your views come from replay, how do you think watching two minutes of dead air at the start of your live is for their viewing experience? If they are generous they will skip forward to find out when you start talking, if they are a regular person they will probably just get bored and find something else to watch.

Who joins your live is something you only have limited control over. Instead, focus on what you can control: delivering an energetic and engaging speech from the moment you press record. When people arrive, they will be more likely to stay as a result.

Not Pausing

This could be a general mistake of speaking, but I notice it's more pronounced on live. It's something I've been working on recently too.

Pausing is a fantastic technique in speaking. It adds suspense, lets a powerful statement sink in, and even gives you time to remember what you're going to say next! On live video, there is a bit of a fear of pausing.

The fear comes from the idea that you have to be saying something for your audience to want to stay live. Think about the example we talked about in the last segment, no one is going to stick around whilst you let the dead air hang. But a pause isn't "dead air", it's a choice to let the silence do the work.

Words are not the way that we earn people's attention, it's the feeling those words conjure. When we ask a question, we spark someone's curiosity. When we pause after that question, the audience gets curious. When we get to the plot twist of a story, the audience gets tense. When we pause at that critical moment, the audience is on the edge of their seats with tension. When the audience is feeling like this, they are not going to leave your live simply because you aren't saying any words.

I've noticed that I pause less and for shorter periods when I'm live. It's odd because it's not as if I don't use pauses in my physical speaking, but I think the lack of feedback on a live can make the pause more intimidating. When you pause in front of a live audience, you get feedback in that pause, they laugh at the punchline of a joke or lean forward to hear what you're going to say next. On live, there is no feedback, it's just you staring back at yourself on the screen. So you just have to get comfortable being in your own silence, which sometimes people find way more intimidating that public speaking! Count to five on your fingers or in your head as you pause to force yourself to hold that silence (trust me, this will not be five seconds, you will count much faster).

Pauses are still just as important on video as they are in front of a physical audience, make sure you are still using them. Your audience isn't going to run away the split second you stop speaking.

Trying To Be Perfect

Similar to pausing, trying to be perfect is a general speaking mistake, but it is particularly counterproductive on live video. The reason that your audience like live videos is because they know it's one take. There's no chance of removing or editing any content, it's there in its original format. This is not something to be frightened by, it's something to embrace.

As we talked about earlier in the book, authenticity is becoming such a buzzword that the word itself almost isn't "authentic" now. In the world of filters and Photoshop, we are crying out for authenticity. But why do we never lead by example?

Live video is where you have the opportunity to be that example. Every mistake and misstep you capture on camera is showing your humanity. And I bet there is little that you can do that is worse than what happened to me on a live video.

My old house was right by the sea, and I decided that to change the energy from constantly doing lives in my indoor office, I would go and sit outside in my garden and have a backdrop of the sea on my live. It was sunny Scottish summer's day (not often do those three words appear together!) and the live was going great. The sun was making me look less like a pasty white vampire than my indoor halo light does and a couple of live viewers were commenting on the beauty of the surroundings. What a fantastic idea.

Then the seagull shat on me. Splat on my shoulder and dribbled down my chest. I shook my fist and called the winged demon a bastard live on air. I then had the presence of mind to look at the camera with a wry smile and remark "least you know this is definitely live!".

I won't say that I loved being the target for a bird bomb, but I did love the nature of that episode. I didn't hold back in calling the seagull a bastard, because that's exactly what I would've done had the camera been off. It was something that I couldn't have anticipated, I've only been hit with bird shit one other time in my life (that was also a seagull, probably partners-in-crime). I, therefore, had to be able to stay composed under a bit of pressure (which after my quick expletive I was able to do) If I'm honest, I probably got a bit of a sympathy vote from the audience at that point as I continued with the live with the poo on full display.

You might not have a live incident quite like this, but you will have one. You cannot compartmentalise real life when you go live. Much more frequent occurrences like the kids asking for dinner, the dog barking at a perceived intruder, or a construction worker deciding this is the best time for a bang and a drill are the types of interruptions you will have to cope with. These are the real-life challenges that people resonate with and they are glad to see when you go live. It doesn't subtract from their experience, it adds to it. So don't lament these imperfections, embrace them. That is what live is all about.

The best thing about the genuineness of live is that it still holds for your replay viewers. Even though they are not watching it live, they know it was recorded live and is the real deal. Apart from the actual live interaction you can have with a live audience,

I think this is the biggest advantage of live video. Your audience perceives it as more authentic. When they see a prerecorded video, they will suspect the practice and refinement that may have gone into it or see the edits you've made. It's not that these are bad, it just creates a slightly different impression. It's for this reason that I keep some imperfections in my prerecorded videos, like saying the wrong thing or tripping over my feet to try and maintain some of that authenticity that comes from a one-take performance.

You now know almost everything there is to know about succeeding on live video. There is one little secret left to share with you though.

I. Revolutions do not wait
II. You have time to pause
III. Perfection will trip you up

Chapter 16

The Secret Apple Trick Almost No One Knows About

Before we finish talking about live video, I want to let you into one last little secret. It's an incredibly useful tool but not always accessible. At the time of writing, it is only available on Facebook Live, and you can only do it on an Apple phone. I do find it annoying that this feature is not universal because it solves a fairly regular problem that I see on live video in particular.

You know when you are driving and you look in your rearview mirror at the car behind you, and their license plate looks like it's written in ancient Greek? That's because your mirror is, surprise surprise, mirroring the text and causing it to appear back to front. (And that's why emergency vehicles write their service in reverse so it appears the right way in your mirror).

Unfortunately, the same thing happens when you are shooting live videos. The reason for this is that you use the selfie camera for live video so that you can read the comments. The selfie camera unfortunately mirrors you on live, which means that any text you try to show on camera is illegible. I see this quite often when someone is trying to show a book to the camera or they maybe have a cue card or whiteboard they are writing key information on. It's simply lost on the audience.

There are two ways around this. The first is to record using the back camera on your phone. The back camera doesn't mirror, so all the writing will appear the correct way round. This does mean that you will not be able to see the screen when you are live, completing robbing you of the interactive element. Not recommended!

My mentor, Karen of the Halo light, taught me the second way around this. Whenever I use this and my halo light at the same time I always extend a little thumbs-up to the sky. There is a setting you can change on Facebook Live. At the top and bottom of your live, you will see there are some icons. The icon we are interested in is the magic wand, which, rather appropriately, is going to help us perform a magic trick. When you click this, a toolbar will appear at the bottom of the screen. These are settings that you can change before and during your live. Most of these are garbage, just putting pointless filters and stupid masks on you. But there is one super useful icon on that toolbar if you are on an Apple phone. It's the screwdriver and spanner crossed over each other.

When you click on that, three further icons appear: a horizontal rectangle with a dotted line down the middle, a vertical rectangle with a dotted line through the middle, and a sun.

Clicking on the sun changes the brightness of the screen, which is useful if you are in a location that is especially light or dark, the default option is normally fine though.

The vertical rectangle is probably more pointless that the filters and masks. What this does is flip the image vertically, so it looks like you're hanging from the ceiling to speak. I see no realistic application for this.

This same trick, however, is much more useful for the third icon, the horizontal rectangle. This will flip the camera so that everything on the left is now on the right and vice versa. This change will only appear to be cosmetic at first. If you part your hair to the right, now it will be parted to the left. If you have a shirt pocket over your left breast, it will now be over your right. Now, hold a book up to the camera.

Apple users rejoice, you can read it now! This icon reverses the mirroring effect and ensures that writing is legible. Before you get too excited, this does come with a side effect. It means that everything you do is mirrored.

Think about standing in front of a mirror and placing your right index finger on the glass. What does your mirrored self do? They place their left index finger on the glass and it looks like you are touching fingers. Try to do this when you change the setting on Facebook Live. Now both of you will put your right index fingers on the screen and they won't be touching but will be on symmetrically opposite sides of the screen. This small discrepancy becomes more pronounced the more you gesture and move. Your avatar will be doing the mirrored opposite of what you do. If you try to point to something over your shoulder, you will end up pointing over the wrong shoulder because you forget to account for the fact that what you are seeing on the screen is swapped over. It can be quite a disorientating experience and break the flow and coherence of your speaking.

For that reason, I suggest you take advantage of the fact that you can change this setting during your live, as well as before it. If the only reason you need the mirror is to show a book at one point of your speech, make the switch at that point in the speech, show the book, say your piece on it, and switch back. If you are usually writing consistently (e.g. presenting with a whiteboard) then try and use more "back and forth" gestures rather than "side to side" as the mirror discrepancy won't be as obvious.

Equally, perhaps you just have to speak as all non-Apple users would, with writing mirrored. If you briefly show a book with the writing the wrong way round, it's not the end of the world. If you are planning a text-heavy speech, then maybe you need to consider filming that as a prerecorded video (or go live using Zoom, which doesn't suffer from the mirroring effect).

Live video is a fantastic medium for connecting with your audience in real-time and creating an intimate, genuine environment in which to communicate. With the tips we've covered, you can go live on your platform of choice and start to build closer relationships with your audience and have more of an impact on their lives.

1.   Ensure your audience can read your revolutionary text

It Is Declared!

Living For Live

The revolution has many branches. The first is Social Media Live. In this third declaration, you have learned how to reach your audience in new ways by using the live stream functions that most social media now offer. If it's good enough for world leaders, it's good enough for you!

Live is a playground to have fun and explore. No one expects you to be perfect on live, in fact, that's what your audience will come to love!

In this declaration, you have learned about the key fundamentals of creating live video, such as recognising the need to appeal to both live and replay audiences and how to generate interaction that both sets of audiences will engage in.

Although both audiences have to be catered for, you do want some kind of live audience with you, otherwise, you are just standing in a room speaking to yourself whilst being recorded. Examples of ways to improve live attendance include scheduling your live and getting the duration of your live in the "Goldilocks Zone".

You also learned how to avoid some of the live mistakes that will cause your revolution to stumble, such as waiting for people to join, not pausing, or trying to be perfect. Neither will you get caught out by not knowing about the secret Apple Trick!

Now that you've gotten to grips with the first major medium of virtual speaking, it's time to explore the next. The Revolution continues.

Declaration Four

Be YOU-nique On YouTube

If you are a fellow nerd, then you'll know that May the 4th is Star Wars Day ("May the Forth be with you"). On this day you are usually expecting some new announcement or trailer to be released for the next Star Wars project. In 2020, May the 4th dropped something a little different.

"Plandemic" definitely wasn't a Star Wars movie, although it was in the same genre of Science Fiction. This 26-minute film racked up millions of views in a short space of time, despite making claims with either little, no, or even opposing evidence (if you fancy some light reading you can consult these references[18][19][20][21]). Smarter people than me have gone through the process of refuting the narrative of Plandemic, but what we're more interested in here is why the video went viral (I promise I'm only going to use that one once!).

Firstly, the video was well produced, unlike some of the other misinformation videos floating around at the time, it didn't

[18] Funke, D. (2020). "Fact-checking 'Plandemic': A documentary full of false conspiracy theories about the coronavirus". *PolitiFact*. Poynter Institute. Retrieved June 15, 2022.

[19] Maxmen, A. and Mallapaty, S. (2021). "The COVID lab-leak hypothesis: what scientists do and don't know". *Nature*. 594, 313–315.

[20] Richardson, I. (2020). "Fact check: Is US coronavirus death toll inflated? Experts agree it's likely the opposite". *USA Today*. Retrieved June 15, 2022.

[21] Wolff, G. (2020). "Influenza vaccination and respiratory virus interference among Department of Defense personnel during the 2017–2018 influenza season". *Vaccine*. 38 (2), 350–354.

look like it was filmed in a basement by a crackpot. Disinformation researcher Erin Gallagher notes that the video's professionally crafted atmosphere, cinematography, and ominously dramatic score made the film look like a legitimate documentary and thus made its claims sound true.[22] Science journalist Tara Haelle observed that it successfully utilises various aspects of persuasion, such as an apparently trustworthy and sympathetic narrator, appealing to emotion, and a rhetorical device known as the "Gish Gallop", where you overload someone with an excessive number of arguments so that it makes it difficult to refute them all. In addition, it was published at a time when audiences were experiencing uncertainty and anxiety and were extremely receptive to someone telling them that they had all the answers.[23]

The first thing that we can learn as virtual speakers from Plandemic is that if something looks the part, we automatically give it more credibility, even if there is no substance behind the veneer. The second thing we can learn is how video virality (sorry, couldn't help myself) works.

Plandemic benefited from what is known as a "Censorship backfire", where trying to hide something just brings more attention to it. Soon after its release, Facebook, YouTube, Vimeo, and Twitter all made decisions to partially or fully censor it. By the time the video was removed from Facebook alone, it had been watched 1.8 million times, had attracted 17,000

[22] Wilson, J. and Gallagher, E. (2020). "Plandemic: how the debunked movie by discredited researcher Judy Mikovits went viral". *The Guardian*. Retrieved June 16, 2022.

[23] Haelle, T. (2020). "Why It's Important To Push Back On 'Plandemic'—And How To Do It". *Forbes*. Retrieved June 16, 2022.

comments, and had been shared nearly 150,000 times.[24] That is no longer something you can hide, and all the censorship did was feed the narrative of a "global elite", or "deep state" run by "Big Pharma" and "Big Tech". As someone with a Master's in Science, I find misinformation and pseudoscience deeply frustrating but I know that the only way to stop it is to give people the tools to understand basic cognitive fallacies and have foundational scientific literacy. Censorship doesn't achieve that and what Big Tech does have to answer for are their algorithms.

The reason why Plandemic was censored is because the algorithms feed the fire of misinformation: they give you more of what you want to see. So when people watch Plandemic, they are led down the rabbit hole with a starter of anti-vax and climate change denial, given a main course of crystal healing remedies and Flat Earth, and finish with a dessert of Holocaust Denial and the New World Order. People buy into misinformation because they aren't given an alternative by Social Media algorithms. The better solution would have been to plaster suggested videos around Plandemic that refute the claims and outline why they are inaccurate, then you teach people how to spot misinformation in the future, rather than just try to hide it from them. But Big Tech isn't going to cut off the hand that feeds them by creating algorithms that give you what you DON'T want to see.

Therefore, the second thing that we can learn from Plandemic is the power of the algorithms. In this case, they allowed misinformation to get a stronger foothold, but the algorithms are neutral. They will spread positive messages in the same way that they spread damaging ones. If you have an

---

[24] Andrews, T. (2020). "Facebook and other companies are removing viral 'Plandemic' conspiracy video". *The Washington Post*. Retrieved June 16, 2022.

important message that helps a lot of people, your message will be spread in the same way.

I believe you are a good person who wants to spread a positive message. I trust that you are someone with integrity who wants to influence people for good reasons. I hope you don't make videos like Plandemic, but I think it would be foolish not to learn the lessons of what made Plandemic a successful video. Looking the part and playing the algorithm are not bad things, they can just be used in bad ways.

This declaration is all about learning how to use YouTube as a virtual speaker. Similar to how I used "Facebook Live" as a catch-all for "Live Video" in Declaration Three, so too will I use "YouTube" as a catch-all for "Pre-recorded video". YouTube is the biggest video platform and offers some unique benefits as a result, but the principles we talk about will apply to any video you first record and then post on similar video-centred platforms like Vimeo, or post on multi-purpose platforms like Facebook and LinkedIn.

Pre-recorded video has some key differences from a live video which we will explore in the following chapters.

Chapter 17

The Culture Of YouTube

The YouTube comment section seems to have earned a reputation that is only partly justified. Maybe it's just the subject area I like to peruse but I don't see the vitriol that is supposed to have originated on YouTube. Usually, people are just thankful for a video that has helped them or entertained them. Those reactions are key to explaining the benefit of YouTube and how you build a community there.

I'm sure the mudslingers have a special swamp of YouTube that they like to roll around in but most people are coming to YouTube for two reasons: to find the solution to a specific problem, or to entertain themselves. As a virtual speaker, you can accommodate both of these desires, but you have to think about them in different ways.

Solving A Problem

Imagine that there is something in the house that needs fixing and you want to save money hiring someone to do it, where would you go to learn how to save yourself some money? Or you have a hot date coming over and you want to make a dinner that is slightly more exciting than Mac and Cheese. Where do you go for your inspiration?

You'd go to YouTube, wouldn't you? It's the one-stop shop for any kind of video tutorial, and this highlights the first key reason that people go to YouTube: to find answers to a specific problem. It's your job as a speaker to know or find out, what problems your audience is looking to solve. What would they type into that search bar on YouTube? Here's what my audience might be typing:

"How to speak confidently on camera"
"How to structure a webinar"
"How to engage your audience on Zoom"

What phrase do you see coming up consistently? "How to". "How to" is the magic phrase that signals "I have a problem, who will solve it for me". You can be that who. If your video can solve that problem for the audience, who do you think will be at the forefront of their mind next time they have a similar problem? When you keep on solving problems for your audience, you will become their go-to expert for that topic.

All this sounds wonderful and simple in theory, but there are some big caveats to explore. Firstly, you aren't the only person who has the bright idea to solve someone's problem with a YouTube video. Take one of the search terms I listed above "How to speak confidently on camera". Type that into YouTube and see how many videos show up. Are any of mine on there? Nope. There are channels with larger audiences and more views that come up first. This is the first obstacle you have to work around: the common problems are already saturated with answers. Type in "how to get a 6-pack", "how to start a business" and "how to have better sex" to see how many results appear for common searches. Good luck trying to get your material seen in that noise. The audience is going to trust the channels that have the most subscribers and click on the videos that have the most views.

This doesn't mean you can't help people with their problems, it just means you need to be more specific with the problems you help them with. Consider three problems below.

"How to start a business"
"How to start an online business"
"How to start an online business for less than $100"

They are essentially the same problem, but the more specific the problem, the less competition you have. If you can help someone start an online business for less than $100, there's no need for you to compete with brick-and-mortar businesses or big tech funded by venture capitalists and/or trust funds. The key to getting your work in front of people searching for solutions is to be more specific about the problem you solve and to solve problems that have less competition. Part of the reason I have specialised in helping people with virtual speaking is that there are far fewer people solving this problem than physical public speaking. Fewer people are searching for a solution to this problem, but they are more likely to find me as a result (look at you reading this book for example!).

The second consideration is that when people are in problem mode, they are looking for quick solutions. If given the choice between a 5-minute video and a 60-minute video, they are going to opt for the 5-minute video, even if the 5-minute solution doesn't solve the problem as effectively as the 60-minute one could.

They are also going to have a short attention span. They want to quickly get to the "how to" part of the video. If they aren't getting clear instructions that they can follow and see the problem improving, they are going to give up on the video and try another. They will listen to you if you can solve the problem quickly but will ditch you if you are taking too long.

Therefore, the first two focuses that your YouTube videos need to have is that they solve specific problems and do so as quickly and efficiently as possible. You should have videos that focus on a single problem at a time and provide guidance to solve it. You don't go on YouTube to learn the ancient art of Persian spices, you go to find out how to make one curry. When you've made a few curries that you like, then maybe you take the time to study your spices in more detail. The first way to make your YouTube channel a success is to help your audience solve problems.

Browsing For Entertainment

You've got an hour to kill. You're watching the oven (perhaps after following a YouTube recipe!), running a bath, or doing the ironing. You decide to open YouTube and see if there's anything you can watch.

This time, you don't head straight to the search bar. You have no clear objective in mind. "How to pass the time" or "How to solve boredom" aren't search terms that people type into YouTube. Instead, they look at the home page. On the home page are recently posted videos from channels that you subscribe to, and suggested videos based on your interests.

For example, if you were on my homepage, the videos you see there are techno DJ sets, rugby highlight videos, and Star Wars fan theories because that is what I predominantly watch on YouTube. These are my viewing habits when I don't have an obvious problem to solve. Crucially, it means I'm more likely to watch another techno, rugby, or Star Wars video, because, as we talked about in the previous chapter, the algorithm wants to feed me more of what I like. This is good news for a content creator in any of these three areas. I'm more likely to come across their video because they make something I enjoy.

This is the second key need that you fulfil for your audience, you provide entertainment through a subject they are interested in. This is a different viewing experience from when your audience is trying to solve a problem. In this scenario, they are pushed for time and want the specific answer as quickly as possible. You have a short time to earn their attention and prove yourself to them. If your video doesn't seem to be going anywhere, they are going to go back to the search results and find something else.

When they are browsing, they are in a different mindset. They are drawn by a picture and caption rather than views and subscribers. They don't have as much of a bias towards shorter videos (in fact they might be looking for something that can specifically take up an hour!) and they will give your video much more of a chance to develop its ideas and themes.

The second way you can build a YouTube audience is by providing entertainment for browsers. You provide deeper, slower content that people absorb at a gentler pace.

Of the two, you are going to probably be providing more "solution-based" videos. Most virtual speakers will be speaking on a topic that more naturally lends itself to this format, and we will cover a framework in a later chapter that allows you to maximise the effectiveness of such videos. But it's important to consider the role of long-form video. My four most watched YouTube videos are all longer than 45 minutes. I have more short-form videos to attract people to what I do, and then longer videos to provide them with a richer experience. You want to make sure you are catering to both types of YouTube audiences.

Now that you know what types of videos to film, let's look at a framework that will help you film your videos.

I. Revolutions solve problems
II. Revolutionaries want to be entertained

Chapter 18

The Carmichael Framework

Most of my video career was just a "turn on the camera and see what happens" affair. I would share an anecdote that I had found interesting, make a distinction I thought was important, and teach 3-5 tips to help improve "x". I didn't really have a framework that I would follow each time to give me some structure and consistency. Therefore some of my videos worked well, others not so much.

That changed when I listened to Brendon Burchard, the man who inspired me to begin speaking in the first place, interview YouTuber Evan Carmichael. Carmichael grew his channel by creating compilations of wisdom from leaders and high achievers e.g. "Bill Gates Top 10 Rules for Success" (at the time of writing this video has 4.6M views). In this interview, Carmichael shared the 8-step framework that he used to help make these videos as successful as they are. When I employed this framework, I noticed a consistent rise in the views of my videos in the region of 25-33%. It didn't require me to speak very differently, just be more thoughtful about how I was structuring what I was speaking about. With credit to Evan Carmichael, I'm going to share this structure with you here, outline how I employ it and give some ideas to help you adapt it for your videos.

1: State A Contrarian Belief

We've already talked about the importance of starting your video with a hook. Stating a belief, contrarian or otherwise, is one such form of a hook. The power of the contrarian belief is that it simultaneously acts as an impactful statement and an intriguing question. Consider an example that I might use below.

"You don't need to be an extrovert to be a great speaker".

With that one statement, I simultaneously set out the stall for what the video is going to be about (introverts can be great speakers), but there is also an embedded question there for the audience (why doesn't being an extrovert automatically make you a good speaker?). Your contrarian belief should challenge an assumption and act as a little jolt to capture your audience's attention. If they assumed that all good speakers are extroverts (as many people do) then your first statement creates a bit of cognitive dissonance for them that they then have to try and resolve by watching more of your video.

2: Give Context For The Belief

In step one you've captured their attention, now you need to earn their continued attention. It's easy to be brash or controversial to force someone's attention. I'm sure many a clickbait article or video has ensnared you this way and then you've departed in a huff. So you need to back up your contrarian belief. To continue from my previous example, my next statement would be:

"Did you know that 50% of TED speakers describe themselves as introverts?"

Now the audience knows I'm not just blowing them full of empty hype. One of the most prestigious stages in the world has been graced by thousands upon thousands of introverts. Now the audience knows you can back up your statement, the next thing they want to know is...

3: What The Audience Needs To Do

...how they can do it too. When you dispel a belief that was potentially holding them back, they want to be let off the reins and head off in the new direction you've told them about. So give them the outline of what they need to do. This is where you make the promise to them about what they are going to learn in this video and how it is going to help them embark in this new direction.

4: Share A Story That Provides Context To The Subject Matter

Those first three steps are pretty rapid fire. I often only have a single sentence for each, and it doesn't take me longer than 60 seconds to complete. You have to quickly demonstrate to your audience why it's worth watching your video. When you do, you then have earned the right to spend a little more time fleshing things out.

This is where step 4 comes in. You now share a story that provides the context to the point you are trying to make. This could be a personal story or anecdote. It could be a case study or client experience. It could be a current affair or a historical event. Stories provide the platform for meaning and rather than just diving into teaching points, you want to demonstrate the transformational effect of those teaching points. When your audience understands the journey they can embark on, then they will be ready to book their transportation.

5: Teaching Point #1

Their transportation begins with your first teaching point. Theoretically, each teaching point could take as long as you want it to. Your video could be an hour long with teaching points of 15-20 minutes or 5 minutes with snappy teaching points of 30-60 seconds. Some channels specialise in bitesize learning, other channels specialise in deep learning. It's really up to the personal style and brand you are aiming to establish. For most of my YouTube videos, my teaching points are 2-3 minutes long which keeps my videos in a "Goldilocks Zone" of 10-15 minutes.

6: Teaching Point #2

After your first point, teach another one.

7: Promotion

You've given your audience some good stuff so far. Now take a pause. Your video isn't going to make the Unifying Theory of Everything. There's more they will want to learn and hopefully, they want to learn it from you.

At this point in the video, direct your audience to a resource you have where they can learn more. The default promotion I have on my videos is directing people toward my Facebook Group "Rise and Inspire Speakers". In some videos, I direct people towards my books (maybe that's how you've ended up reading this right now!). On some videos, I direct people towards some of my paid programs, although this is less regular because people probably aren't going to hire me as a coach when I've taught them two tips on body language, no matter how good those tips are!

Whatever it might be, give your viewers somewhere they can go after the video if they want to learn more, which you know they do since they are watching your video!

8: Teaching Point #3 And Conclusion

To show them you are good value, then give them your third teaching point and wrap up what you've talked about in your video. You can remind them of your teaching points, but also remind them about the first three points you made. Remind them that they can be a great public speaker even if they are an introvert, as long as they follow the three teaching points. Give them a spark of inspiration to send them on their way, which could be to watch your next video or access that resource you share with them.

How To Film Using This Framework

With this framework, I write down the three statements I want to make for the first three points. I don't try to memorise the script, I just practice it a couple of times until I feel I've got the sentiment of my ideas correct then film the first three steps in one take. Next, I think about the story I'm going to share and then turn on the camera again to film that. Then I choose a keyword for each of my three teaching points (e.g. "camera", "gestures") and film each of those separately. I then have a separate piece of promo footage for my Facebook group/book/ program already prepared.

When I get to the editing room I, therefore, have six pieces of footage (The first three steps are one clip, then each step after that has its own clip). I trim the bookends of dead air off each clip then cut from one to the other, with no fancy transitions or whizz-bang effects. You may find this a little less intimidating than filming the whole video in one take and I've also found it quicker and easier to insert my promotional footage into the video when I have a clear distinction between steps 6 and 8, rather than scrolling through the video file trying to find the exact timepoint where I finish Teaching Point #2 and start Teaching Point #3.

You'll remember that earlier in the book I talked about filming your videos in one take and this approach may seem to contradict that. Firstly, I still encourage you to film the different steps in one take and without a script using keywords to guide you. Secondly, I encourage you for other forms of video, such as social media, that you still adhere to the one-take principle. Of course, you can still use this framework and film in one take if you want to really embed that principle first (if you are just starting out, you might not have anything to promote in Step 7 and have nothing to edit in there).

This framework has not only helped me improve engagement on my videos and subscribers to my channel, but it has also led to more people following up with that promotional step of joining my Facebook Group, buying my book, or even signing up for some of my programs. Thanks, Evan!

Now that you know a framework for filming your YouTube videos, let's go into a little more detail on the production processes for your videos.

I.   Revolutionaries are contrarian
II. State strong beliefs
III. Show people what they need to do
IV. Share stories that capture the message
V.   Teach three things
VI. Promote your revolution

Chapter 19

Production Value

We had to give it to Plandemic on looking the part right? Given that video is such a visual experience, it makes sense that how it looks plays a big part in how it's received. With that said, you are not a one-person Hollywood studio. You don't have to be producing a cinematic experience for every little video you film. Even if you have some kind of team helping you out (someone you hire or a strongarmed tech-savvy child!) it still isn't necessary to put every possible bell and whistle on a video just because you can. As the saying goes, sometimes less is more.

When I first started to get used to editing my videos in iMovie, I got excited by all the new features I was learning. It was taking me more and more time to put a video together, far more time than actually filming it thanks to my one-take filming method. At the time I was still speaking around my regular job and I had to ask myself whether hours in the editing studio were the best use of the limited free time I had. I wasn't aiming for a career in video production, I was aiming for one in public speaking.

That said, learning how to use all the features does give you the option, for special videos and given the right context, to employ some of the "bells and whistles" should you wish. There are two main areas of production value you need to think about.

The first is your recording set-up. This is literally where you are filming your videos and some of the visual and audio considerations before you press record.

The second is what you do in the editing studio. I would say that the only — almost — essential piece of editing with a raw video file is learning to chop off the start of the file before you start speaking and chop off the end of the file when you are pressing the button to stop recording. But in the beginning, you can get away with even not doing that, but it does portray an amateurish quality that you won't want to continue with for long. All the other editing options are just that: optional. I'm sure this will please some of the Technophobes reading this!

Let's start by considering the important factors as you record your video.

Recording Set Up

Whilst I'm a big advocate for simplifying the video process in the beginning by just pulling out your phone or sitting in front of your webcam and speaking, you do want to add a bit of refinement over time as you get more confident and comfortable in front of the camera. Let's think about how you want to set up your own little home studio for filming (by "home studio" we are talking about corners of the office, garden benches, and sofas!). There are three things to consider here: lighting, background, and acoustics.

Lighting

Your first consideration is lighting. Here you have two choices: natural or artificial.

You might think that natural is better but this isn't always the case. If you film outside on a bright day where the sun is high rather than at an awkward angle, yes it looks great. If you are filming near a window that is bathing you in strong natural light, yes that's grand. The issue with natural light is, of course, that we don't control it. A clear spring or summer's day, whether you are outside or inside, will give you nice lighting. However, in the autumn or winter when the sun is lower and weaker, or the sun frequently has clouds passing over it, will give you patchy light. I do enjoy getting a good outdoors video on a sunny day, but you really can't rely on that as a long-term video strategy.

Therefore, artificial is likely to be a better bet in terms of consistency. However, bad artificial light is maybe worse than bad natural light. A single energy-saving lightbulb dangling from the roof will give you an awful image. Domestic lights just don't cut it. You will need lighting that is designed for filming like halo lights and light boxes.

When I first started filming videos, I did rely on natural light. In the two apartments I lived in at the beginning of my speaking journey, I had a couch near a large window. These windows would give me enough exposure to natural light to do an acceptable video. That being said, it shortened my filming window in the winter months as I had to do the filming right in the middle of the day, as the sunlight simply wasn't strong enough at any other time. If you have a good source of natural light in your home, then you can certainly start your filming there.

Now I have strong artificial lights, which gives me more flexibility. I use them when filming inside even during summer time as it gives me a uniform lighting pattern and they make filming so much easier during the darker periods of the year.

If you are blessed enough to have a good source of natural light in your home, then you can certainly wing it there, to begin with. If you don't of course nothing is stopping you from still filming the videos. It's far better to just get in the game than use "not having the right lighting" as procrastination. Still, you may want to invest in at least a cheap halo light/light box to get you started.

Background

Similar to lighting, you have two choices here: minimal or designed.

Minimalism involves a blank backdrop like a white wall. This type of wall reflects light well and it brings you as a speaker into focus. The advantage of this is that not everyone is blessed with a nice environment to film in, but most of us can engineer a blank wall somewhere in the home. The slight issue with it is that it can look somewhat "clinical" and in bad lighting, it doesn't have anything going for it.

On the other hand, you can go designed, where your background contains a lot of your personality and brand. You might have a banner with your business logo on it. You might have a neatly arranged bookshelf. You might have some plants. You might have a desk with a leather-bound journal and a pot of tea. It's really up to you. I think that done well, this helps your video to stand out. The only issue is that it sometimes isn't appropriate for all the types of video you might be filming. Sitting at your desk with your steaming pot of tea is great for a conversational Facebook Live, but perhaps for an interactive Zoom workshop being stuck at your desk might be restrictive.

Whichever you choose, try and avoid the middle ground between these two, which is just "cluttered". Although the pandemic was a great leveller in terms of people's home environment, you probably don't want to have your laundry sitting in view of your long-term filming location, have piles of boxes visible in a corner, or a single random picture sitting on your otherwise blank wall, for example.

For beginner speakers, it's usually easier to find or create somewhere that is clear and blank, rather than try and design something fancy. Find that stretch of blank wall in a private room that doesn't require shifting pieces of furniture everywhere to clear it. That's enough to get you started.

Acoustics

The final consideration is sound. Generally speaking, your device's microphone is going to be good enough for this, certainly to begin with. End of discussion.

There are a couple of caveats to consider here. If you are using your webcam on a laptop or desktop that maybe isn't the most up-to-date, then it may have a shoddy built-in microphone. This is occasionally the case with phones but less often. The solution in both cases is often just plugging in some headphones like the Apple Earbuds we've talked about before and that solves the problem.

You may also be trying to film in a room that you can't help being noisy. You are right next to a busy street in the city centre or close to a railway (I am just now!). In this case, you may want to again think about bringing a microphone closer to your mouth to pick up more of your voice and less of the white noise. Headphones could work here again or a clip-on microphone would do the job too.

In summary, you can start filming using a blank backdrop with decent natural light and no microphone. Everything else beyond that is an optional extra that you can add along the way. Don't overcomplicate the process and get stuck in the web of procrastination.

Editing Studio

After you've filmed your video, you can then think about how you are going to spruce it up in the editing studio. Remember that I said earlier that I think the only essential piece of editing is chopping off the dead air at the start and end of the file. Everything else we are going to outline after this is a fun optional extra that you can employ as and when you think it might be appropriate.

Cuts

Once you learn how to trim off the start and end of your raw video file, you have essentially learned how to do a basic cut. A "cut" is where you splice two different pieces of footage together, i.e. it's not a continuous shot.

If you watched films in the black and white era, they use very few cuts. They generally have a fixed camera and the characters move around using that one camera as their reference point. The camera often only moves when the location in the film changes. Modern films, by contrast, use rapid cuts, often only showing a second of a shot before moving to another camera to show a different character's face, a new angle of the room, or flash to events in a different location. Recent films like "1917" actually buck this trend by utilising an almost continuous camera shot.

Our world of virtual speaking is much more "Casablanca" than "Fast and Furious". You will usually only have one camera when filming and you won't be acting out dramatic and dynamic scenes. When you are broadcasting live, you don't have the option to make cuts, but you can with prerecorded video. You'll notice that a lot of YouTube influencers, even when just filming in one location on one camera, make very fast cuts across their video, sometimes cutting a single sentence. I don't recommend that, because we're speakers, not YouTube personalities and we're filming for a different purpose. Nonetheless, it does illustrate that we can choose to make an occasional cut on our speaker videos.

The most common reason for beginners to use cuts is when they forget something or flub a line. I encourage beginner speakers to just shoot a continuous piece of film to get used to the "one take" reality of a broadcast, and then go and tidy up that take in the editing room. You can cut out blank bits where you forgot what you were going to say or the footage where you said too much and repeated yourself or went off on a tangent.

Then you just piece together where you stopped saying something that made sense with where you started speaking sense again.

Cuts can also be used a little more artistically. You may film in different locations and make the cut when you move. For example, if you were filming an exercise video you would make the cuts when you've moved to different pieces of equipment in a gym. Alternatively, for a nutrition video, you might film yourself buying ingredients at a market and then cut to preparing them in the kitchen. You can even just use cuts to separate different sections of your video. This is the approach that I've settled into now for my YouTube videos, cutting between each stage of the Carmichael Formula.

In the beginning, use cuts when you have big sections of dead air in your videos, or you end up speaking a heap of nonsense for a couple of minutes. Keep your editing touch light at the beginning of your journey though, remember we are seeking to embrace the imperfection in the beginning, not trying to hide it. Don't try and cut out every single blemish, real or imagined, just the clunky bits that don't add value.

Captions

When I first started filming videos, there were no captions AI on any of the major social media platforms. When your video sits on a social media feed, it is automatically put on mute. This means that people don't know what you're saying until they click on it. If the video description and image weren't compelling enough, they wouldn't click on it. Alternatively, if they are in a space where they are unable to play the sound, such as public transport, then they wouldn't be able to access your video even if they wanted to watch it. And of course, the videos were not accessible for deaf people either.

To put subtitles onto your video, you needed to integrate your video with a special 3rd party AI provider (I never learned how to do this) or add your own on your editing platform. Manually adding captions for every sentence you say was just unfeasible, but you could add the first 30 seconds of speech to try and grab people's attention and have them click on your video to unmute and listen to the rest.

This has now changed completely, as all the major social media platforms automatically add subtitles to your videos that autoplay when muted and can be turned on when unmuted. This is a game changer and has taken away the main reason why you would want to add captions.

Captions are still something you can consider if you want certain keywords or phrases to pop on the screen as you speak, but this is a feature I utilise very rarely now.

Backing Music

The final touch-up you may want to consider in the editing studio is backing music. Similar to the other editing tools, this turns into a balance between value-added versus time expended. For the first year or two of shooting videos, I was putting backing tracks on them, before recognising that I was spending just as much time sourcing good copyright-free music as I was shooting the videos. Similar to captions, this is only something I use for special occasions.

That being said, having some kind of intro and outro music that you play on all your videos may be something that helps your videos stand out and showcase your personality without being too time-consuming.

To summarise again, you may want to employ some cuts here and there in your videos, but features like captions and backing music may be something you happily never use.

Now that you've made the necessary adjustments to your video in the editing studio, let's look at getting this video onto YouTube and some of the important steps you want to take to maximise the reach of your videos when you post them.

I.   *Virtual speakers need good lighting*
II.   *Keep your background uncluttered*
III. *Ensure good acoustics*
IV.   *Cut what's not needed*
V.   *Make sure your videos are accessible to all who may wish to join the movement*
VI.   *Music can inspire your revolution*

Chapter 20

Getting On YouTube

Now your video is polished, it's time to publish. There are some important features of the YouTube platform that give you the best possible chance of your video being seen and building a following. Unlike the editing, you want to make sure you are employing these tactics, I'm kicking myself for spending half a decade not doing one of them!

Let's cover each of them one by one.

Title

The title is the most important part of your video (sadly, even more important than the actual content!). The title is really what determines if someone watches your video. Remember earlier we talked about viewer behaviour on YouTube: whether they are browsing or searching, the title is one of the most important factors in why they ultimately click on your video. No click, no view. It doesn't matter how good the video is if no one clicks on it.

The title needs to earn your audience's attention. Don't call your video something generic like "Public Speaking Tips" or "My Story". The title needs to be catchy, intriguing, and useful without being clickbait. You offer the solution to a problem your audience needs to solve or spark their curiosity about something they want to learn more about. You want it to be fairly short and snappy as if your title is too long, YouTube won't show the whole title until someone actually clicks on the video (and they are less likely to click if they aren't sure what the video is about). The exact length may change with platform updates, but at the time of writing YouTube will show the full title if it is 100 characters or less, which is quite generous and will accommodate most punchy statements or questions.

Video Description

The video description is the text that goes below your video. You might ask why this is important. If you're anything like me, you hardly ever read the video descriptions on YouTube right? Video descriptions play more of a part before you watch the video.

This is because video descriptions play a role in the SEO (Search Engine Optimisation) of your videos. For those of you who don't know about the dark arts of SEO, this means how likely it is that a search term (e.g. "how to be a better virtual speaker") will find your content. I personally think that SEO is vastly overhyped, especially by people who want to sell $2,000 courses on how to "hack SEO". It used to be that you could put "public speaking" on your website 1,000 times and when someone typed "public speaking" into Google your website would be top of the results because it had the highest number of the term "public speaking".

The algorithms are way smarter than that now and employ a constellation of search terms and keywords to stop this SEO spamming. People are always looking for ways to game the system rather than just stick to solid principles and producing good content.

That being said, your video description plays into the constellation of keywords the algorithm looks for. If my video on public speaking includes related search terms like "confidence", "body language", and "speech structure", then it will get a small boost in the rankings compared to a video that doesn't include these terms. This boost, as I said, is vastly overhyped, but it's still something to think about.

Writing a video description for YouTube is not just useful for minor SEO benefits, but it also makes crossposting the video so much easier. This is where I think the description is far more useful. When I share the video on LinkedIn or to my email list, I then just copy and paste the video description which means I don't have to write multiple descriptions for the same video.

A final factor to consider with a video description is it allows you to post links. If you want to direct people to your website, book on Amazon, or even another video on YouTube, then you can provide the link in an easy-to-access place in the video description.

End Screen

This is a feature I didn't notice or understand for half a decade of posting videos on YouTube. When I started using it, I doubled my subscribers in 12 months. It's fair to say I'm facepalming quite hard that I neglected this for so long.

When you post your video to YouTube, you will get the opportunity to decide on features such as the thumbnail (the picture you see before you click on the video), video description, and subtitles. One feature I just skipped over in this process was called "End Screen". As the name suggests, this gives you different options to add something to your video as it approaches the end such as suggesting more videos or directing people to subscribe to your channel.

Directing people to subscribe to your channel. Is it any wonder that when I took the simple step of reminding people to subscribe to my channel at the end of a video they had clearly enjoyed (they wouldn't have watched to the end if they didn't) that they might go ahead and subscribe? And providing them with another video to watch would then increase the views on my videos because they enjoyed the first one and wanted more.

It is painfully obvious as I spell it out on the page now, so don't be as blind as I was. Get that end screen up on your videos, about 20 seconds before it finishes. Your subscribers and views will go up.

Thumbnails

Before we wrap up this segment, I'll go into more depth about one other feature you can set up before posting your video: the thumbnail. If you go to an established YouTube channel, you will see that they put a lot of work into designing a thumbnail with bright colours, logos, screenshots, and text. This looks nice and it's certainly an aspiration for your channel.

My only concern with thumbnails is thinking about when you are starting out, and when you are the sole employee of your enterprise, is it the best use of your time to design a thumbnail? I personally still like the minimal approach of just using a still from the video footage and sometimes these can actually be quite amusing and catch the eye. Especially if I have been filming in a nice location I like to let the environment do the talking. At the start of your journey, I would rather you spent your time filming videos than editing and designing them, so thumbnails for me fall into the "nice to have" rather than "need to have" category.

After covering all the production processes of your videos, let's now wrap up this declaration on YouTube by talking about how YouTube factors into your long-term plans.

I. *Write a catchy title*
II. *Describe your video vividly*
III. *Make sure you add an end screen*
IV. *Capture people with a thumbnail*

Chapter 21

The Gift That Keeps On Giving

Once your YouTube channel is set up, it starts to generate momentum for you. The accumulation of videos, subscribers and views are all incredibly helpful for you not just in terms of improving your speaking, but feeding into your business as well. Let's look at three ways that YouTube becomes the gift that keeps on giving.

Monetisation

YouTube is actually unique among the social media platforms in that you get directly paid for being popular. Instagram Influencers are always looking for the latest endorsement and Facebook Gurus have to run ads to their products and services. YouTube actually give you a cut of the ads that get run on your videos by default.

There are a couple of important points to cover here. First, monetisation doesn't activate until you have 1000 subscribers and 4000 hours of view time per month (which doesn't have to come from just subscribers). Second, 1000/4000 doesn't activate the "magic money tree" of YouTube. This is pennies per video to begin with, but as the views build, it's giving you money for something you'd be doing anyway right?

For successful YouTubers, the monetisation alone becomes enough to live on, regardless of the extra endorsements they get or programs they run.

Library And Archive

YouTube is a great way to store all your videos, speeches, workshops and anything else you do as a speaker. It's material that you can pull out months or years after recording it to reshare and repurpose. On the other social media platforms your content can get lost in news feeds or require a ton of scrolling to find it. YouTube is a bit easier as you can list your videos by "oldest" or "most popular" to find them more quickly. If you can remember the video you can also just search for it. If I'm trying to find a body language video I remember filming four years ago I can just search "body language" and it will filter the list down to my videos with that term in the title or video description (remember that SEO!).

This can be as useful as simply looking back on a speech or video from a few years ago to see how far you've come. You may need to remind yourself on concepts you used to talk about years ago but haven't covered for a while (yes you really do forget your own stuff. My clients often quote things to me that I don't remember saying!).

You may also have private workshops or keynotes for paying clients that you don't necessarily want to share for free, but you do want to keep for future use. Rather than getting lost in a forgotten desktop folder or external hard drive, you can store them as an unlisted video on YouTube. That means only people you share the link with can view it. You can use this to send advanced training to clients or to give event organisers footage of your speaking to help them with their hiring decision.

Recycle Content

The biggest bonus of this archive, rather than just having it for your own posterity, is that you can recycle past content to post on your social media channels. You don't have to create new content every day or every week, you can use good videos you've already recorded. Let's say you are fielding a lot of questions on the same topic and you've already shot a video answering those questions. Just share the video you've already recorded and it will get you more views and satisfy your audience. If something comes up in current affairs that you've already got a great video to provide commentary or analysis, share away!

Here's my favourite. If you are on holiday or otherwise engaged and you are too busy to make content or you are choosing to prioritise more important things, then you can just return to a previous "winner" in your content library and schedule that to be shared. This is a video that got a high number of views/likes/comments the first time you shared it. Whenever you share something, only a fraction of your audience ever see it. The average email open rate is around 20%[25], the average organic reach (not supported by ad money) on social media is around 5%.[26] So when you share something "old", 80-90% of

[25] https://influencermarketinghub.com/email-open-rates/. Retrieved 13th July 2022

[26] https://www.ignitesocialmedia.com/social-media-strategy/social-media-organic-reach-2021-who-actually-sees-your-content/. Retrieved 13th July 2022

your audience think it's "new". Additionally, you will always be amassing new followers who aren't aware of your previous material. So whilst I encourage you to be continuously iterating and creating new content, don't always think that "new" equals "best", there's value resting in your content archive.

Whatever social media you may find yourself on as a virtual speaker, what I consider to be the essential platform you must be on is YouTube. This was really the first place that it became feasible to be a virtual speaker and it is a platform that continues to support up and coming virtual speakers. Make sure it is part of your support system too.

I. Revolutions need to be funded
II. Build your archive of revolutionary materials
III. Use winners repeatedly

It Is Declared!

It's Time For More YOU

It was on YouTube that the origins of the Virtual Speakers Revolution can be traced, the ability to truly transmit your speaking across the world was born. Whilst it can be used to amplify misinformation as with "Plandemic", it can also amplify the good stuff you share too.

Understanding the culture of YouTube allows you to cater to your audience's need for education and entertainment and tailor different videos for different purposes.

You have been given a framework that you can use to structure all your videos and improve the engagement with your content and increase the following of your channel.

We went deep into the weeds with production, looking at the key factors to think of when filming, editing, and posting your videos.

Thanks to monetisation, and the reoccurring value of your archive, YouTube is a gift that keeps on giving and it will prove valuable support in your Virtual Speakers Revolution.

There's one final tool to explore. A good revolution needs good resources, and you don't want to join the revolution without knowing how to use this one.

Declaration Five

Get Zappy With Zoom

Each year, in Toastmasters International, there are two biannual contests. The first is the Humorous Speech and Table Topics contest which takes place in the autumn. The second is the Speech Evaluation and International Speech Contest which takes place in the spring.

The International Speech Contest is the big daddy. Whilst the other three contests stop after four rounds, usually at the national level (UK and Ireland for me, for example), the International Speech, as the name suggests, goes all the way to a world final and a World Champion of Public Speaking is crowned each year.

In March 2020, we began the process as usual. I was gutted to not be participating, but after having my panic attacks the previous month, I was trying to ease my workload and give myself time to recover. Putting in practice time for my speech and travelling around the country to compete in contests wasn't going to be healthy for me. If I'd known what was about to happen, maybe I would've had a pop.

We ran the first round of the contest at our club on Wednesday 11th March to determine who our club representative would be for the Speech Evaluation and International Speech contest. One of the big rituals of Toastmasters is shaking hands. When one speaker hands the stage over to another, we shake hands to indicate the transfer is taking place. The government guidance at the time was to avoid this and so instead we were bumping elbows with each other. We made a couple of jokes about how strange this felt. Otherwise, the contest ran as normal. That turned out to be our last physical meeting for about 20 months. Less than two weeks later, we were in lockdown.

The contests continued from that point forward on Zoom, all the way to the World Championship. As I write this in 2022, most of the contest rounds were still held on Zoom this year, but the world semi-finals and finals are being held in person for the first time since 2019, in Nashville, USA.

The 2021 International Speech contest, however, started on Zoom from the very first round and ended on Zoom at the world final. 2021 may prove to be the only year in Toastmasters history that the International Speech contest was hosted entirely online from start to finish.

Verity Price, therefore, may be the only World Champion of Public Speaking who never did the "public" part of public speaking. She won the 2021 World Championship of Public Speaking having never set foot on a physical stage. And she almost didn't enter![27]

After being a Toastmaster for nearly ten years, Price had only entered the contest twice before and had never gotten further than the first couple of rounds. After being pregnant in 2019, Price was thinking of leaving Toastmasters altogether. However, when lockdown hit, she started to watch the online

_____

[27] Interview with Verity Price 15/7/22

contest in 2020, and when she saw the 2020 winner, Mike Carr, crowned online, she got the bug to enter one more time.

She had delivered a speech before in Toastmasters with a message that she felt she wanted to share with the world: "leave the world a better place than you found it". Price describes how from the moment she entered the contest at the beginning of 2021, she was imagining a worldwide audience hearing this message, not necessarily as a world champion, but certainly as a world finalist. Price went through 32 versions of this speech throughout the contests as she honed and refined the essence of what she wanted to capture in this speech. This speech became "The Challenge", a story about her mother's desire to clean up the world, one bit at a time, a speech that took her all the way to the World Finals.

In this contest, you can use the same speech all the way up to the world semi-finals. At the world semi-finals and final, you must deliver two different speeches. You can use the speech that's got you there in the semi-final or final, but not both. Price opted to deliver "The Challenge" in the semi-final, meaning that she had to create a new speech for the final. After finding out that she had qualified, Price started working on her second speech 100 days before the final. Considering one speech was about her mum, she decided it was only fair that her second speech was about her dad.

With "The Challenge", Price had been very clear on the message, but unsure about the content, hence the 32 different editions! With this second speech, she was clear on the content, but unsure of the message. She knew she wanted to tell the story of reading a letter her dad left her after he died, but she struggled to clarify what the take-home message was. After countless practices, numerous pieces of feedback, and extensive coaching, she still couldn't articulate the essence of what she was trying to say. 10 days before the final, she and her coach finally captured it "if you're not happy, write a different story". The speech "A Good Read" was ready for the finals.

Unlike the live format, where you deliver your speeches and hear the results pretty much straight after, the Zoom contests, at the later rounds, have the speeches pre-recorded to avoid technical errors, so Price actually had to wait on the final results for a couple of weeks! After enduring that bubbling tension, she was finally watching the recording at the Virtual Convention. After seeing all the other competitors, she felt she had done the message proud and created a speech good enough to win. After the last finalist's speech was played, the judges' results were announced: Verity Price was the 2021 World Champion.

She was just the 6th woman to win the title and the first champion ever from Africa (Price is a Zimbabwean living in South Africa). She had won entirely using a tool that had come to prominence during the pandemic: Zoom.

When Price and I discussed how speeches were first delivered on camera when lockdown hit, we observed that they were quite rigid. Speakers stood a fixed distance from the camera and were basically "filming a physical speech", rather than delivering a speech designed and adapted for camera. Price admitted this is how she was running the workshops for her business at the time. That changed when she watched the 2020 World Championship final. 1st Place Speaker Mike Carr played with the distance from the camera, telling stories in the past further from the camera then coming closer to tell jokes and emphasise his points, whilst 2nd Place Speaker Linda-Marie

Miller used placards with text to illustrate unconscious bias and racial discrimination. These examples showed Price that there was a better way to deliver speeches than just "recording yourself speaking". In both her speeches "The Challenge" and "A Good Read" she employed the technique of coming closer to the camera and hiding and revealing multiple props.

Price was able to employ a new tool to accomplish a record-breaking goal that she was actively going to resign on in 2019. If it wasn't for Zoom, we'd still be waiting for an African World Champion in Toastmasters. The International Speech Contest is normally dominated by North Americans. I think that's a pretty powerful statement of how much of an equaliser Zoom can be.

Zoom allows anyone to be an expert and reach people anywhere in the world. It is one of my favourite and most versatile tools. When I interviewed Verity Price for this case study, guess which platform we used to connect Scotland and South Africa?

In the following chapters, you are going to learn how to make the most of this amazing platform. You will learn the myriad ways you can use Zoom: it's much more than just a work call platform. Additionally, you will learn how to enhance your speaking using the tools that Zoom provides you and which techniques work best when delivering a speech on Zoom.

Chapter 22

What To Zap

Like all virtual speaking, Zoom has a few nuances and unique features to be mindful of. At the start of the pandemic, I noticed a lot of people were getting more freaked out about Zoom than they needed to. Yes, Zoom does have a lot of features and options, but most of them you don't need to worry about. In this chapter, we are going to break down which features you may want to zap from time to time, and some that you can ignore. After a couple of years of using this platform, you may be familiar with most or all of these features, but you can maybe identify some blind spots with the features or bad habits you might have developed.

Speaker Or Gallery

There are times when you are going to want to see everyone on a Zoom (or at least the 25 people on the first page), and other times when you want to see just one person. This is where the speaker and gallery options come in. Let's look at all the examples of when you might prefer one to the other.

Speaker

The most obvious example of this is when you have one person who is the primary speaker, like a workshop facilitator or keynote speaker. You want to see them as much as you can so you blow up their picture and minimise the rest. Something that a lot of people do is leave the five video boxes down the side or at the top/bottom. If the speaker is really dynamic or there are a lot of visuals and props, I prefer to minimise these videos rather than watch people stroking their cat or picking their nose.

The less obvious example of when to go into speaker view is when YOU are speaking. If you are running something interactive like a workshop, then you will likely want to be on gallery view so that you can see people's responses and call on them to interact and participate.

If you are going to be doing something more one-sided, on the other hand, that gallery may actually prove a distraction. That tendency for the human brain to be attracted to faces means your gaze is always likely to be drawn onto the screen. As we know from our earlier chapter on eye contact, this doesn't give the impression you are looking at your audience, it gives the impression that you are not.

There are certain speeches where I will "pin" myself (if you click on someone's picture and select "pin", their picture will always be "blown up" on your speaker view, even if someone else talks) so I can focus on delivering my speech. I will certainly use interactive techniques like rhetorical questions, answering in the chat box, and addressing "you" so it isn't a monologue, but if I'm not looking for verbal or physical reactions then I sometimes find it easier to keep the screen clear of distractions.

This is a technique you might want to employ if you are working on improving your eye contact with the camera or if you need to focus on your content.

Gallery

I would say that Gallery is more of a "default option" for Zoom. Because Zoom offers the ability for those group dynamics, you want to be delivering speeches in this medium that are more interactive. Unless there is one primary speaker, yourself or someone else, delivering a keynote-style speech, then you probably want to remain on gallery view.

Audio

We know by now the trope of "you're on mute". It seems that after two years this function still sometimes needs to be explained! But rather than waste time on that what I want to cover is your audio quality on Zoom.

If you can, avoid using the default microphone. Most people's laptops don't have a good in-built microphone. Usually, this is easily remedied just by plugging in a pair of Apple headphones. Not only does it improve the quality of your input with the attached microphone, but it also avoids disturbing other people working in your environment (at least when you're not talking. My wife gets disturbed when I talk no matter what device I'm using). When I'm running workshops, I'm usually sitting or standing close enough to the laptop to still remain attached using the headphones.

There may be a time for a particularly dynamic speech or workshop where you can't remain attached to the device. Here you may want to consider a clip-on microphone or lapel mic to keep that audio quality crisp even as you are further away from the microphone.

Recording

This has become one of my favourite features on Zoom and has made my virtual speaking so much more versatile. We'll go into the benefits of the recording feature in the next chapter, but for now, there are two different ways of recording a Zoom session and it's worth covering them both.

Recording To Computer

This option is your default and it should be used on most occasions. After your Zoom session has finished, the recording will process on your computer. How long this takes is entirely dependent on how long you recorded for. A ten-minute speech might only take a couple of minutes. The two-hour workshops that I run for my coaching programs take about 20 minutes. Whilst you are processing the recording, you can't use Zoom until it has finished. This scenario demonstrates the one time you don't want to record to your computer.

Recording To Cloud

The cloud space that you get given on the first tier of paid Zoom isn't much. Since I recommend the first tier of Zoom for most people's needs this is the situation you will generally be faced with. I, therefore, suggest you don't use this option often as you will simply run out of space and you don't want to get caught trying to make a recording and end up losing it because there wasn't enough space to store it. There's one special occasion you should save this for.

Unlike recording to your computer, which as I outlined can take up to 20 minutes for a large file. Recordings get sent to the cloud instantly. That means, if you have back-to-back calls that you also need to record, this is a better option for you.

At the start of the pandemic, I recorded the "Isolation Inspiration Interview" series on my podcast. I released two interviews every week for 12 weeks during the peak of lockdown. These interviews were, of course, recorded ahead of time. I did as many as 4 in one day and they frequently lasted 90 minutes. This meant the recording files were large and I was often jumping straight off one interview onto another. Recording to the cloud made this feasible for me, as I didn't have to delay my next guest because the previous guest's file was still processing. If you find yourself in these back-to-back scenarios, record to the cloud instead.

Interactive Features

There are multiple features on Zoom that can be classed as "interactive". We've touched upon how you might use these in previous chapters, and we'll cover their use a little more in the chapters to come. For now, let's just outline the basic options you have and how to activate them.

Chat Box

This is your simplest and most used form of interaction. Whenever you ask a question, you can collect answers using the chat box. Remember that as well as being used for group communication, you can use it for individual communication as well.

Anyone on a Zoom meeting can be privately messaged by any other member. Someone may want to send you a sensitive question privately rather than publicly and you can answer privately or anonymously. You can also ask everyone in the group to send private feedback to a member in regards to their contribution to a task or activity. For example, when someone delivers a speech on my group coaching calls, I get people to send them feedback as a private message. It can make people more comfortable to give and receive feedback knowing it won't be telegraphed to the whole group.

Share Screen

Along with the chat box, this will probably be your most common interactive feature. It's what you use to share your desktop so that your audience can see slides, a web page, or a document. There's one other feature you can access here which is worth knowing about.

One screen that you can share is a whiteboard. This whiteboard operates as a physical one would. You can draw (simple!) diagrams on it and also write text. If there were moments in a physical meeting where you would be utilising a flipchart or whiteboard, then this is your virtual substitute.

Polls

You can create polls either ahead of time or in the moment to collect audience opinions. When you click poll, you simply write the question and then write down as many options as you need to cover. Everyone in the group can vote, and then you receive the results privately and can choose how to announce them. At many Toastmasters clubs, at each meeting, the "best speaker", "best evaluator" and "best table topics" (improv speaking) are voted for. At physical meetings this is done on pieces of paper, on Zoom, these polls have been an easy substitute.

Breakout Rooms

When you click "Breakout Rooms" you first select how many rooms you want to create. You may just need to split the group in two, in which case you just select "1" (remember you already have one room, the main room). You can create as many of these as you need to split your audience into the required size: groups of 4, 6, 10, etc.

When you have the rooms, you can simply assign people randomly if you just doing a general group activity. However, if people are required to be in specific groups (e.g. "sales team", "IT team") then you can manually assign people and even name the rooms to make the organisation easier.

As the host, you can also move between rooms. This can help you check in on people's progress on a task you may have given them, or offer help and support to multiple groups (think of "moving round the tables" in a physical setting).

What You Hopefully Don't Have To Worry About

There's one feature you should never have to use, but unfortunately, you probably need to know about it.

If you get a "Zoom Bomber", you need to know how to get rid of them. I've had a couple of morons during my time. I've had someone trying to sell cryptocurrency, someone spouting pro-Putin propaganda, and even just someone who refused to stop shouting out and interrupting me. To alleviate yourself and the group of such distractions, simply click on their video and select the "block" option.

If only it were so easy in real life, eh?

What You Definitely Don't Have To Worry About

You know one of the things I'm going to tell you not to worry about already, don't you? After my earlier tirade, you know I'm not a fan of virtual backgrounds, so no need to worry about that or any of the other filters that are available on Zoom (did you see the video of the lawyer in Texas who turned himself into a cat?).

Anything that I haven't mentioned so far, you also don't need to worry about. As you use Zoom more and get more advanced, there are one or two things you may want to play around with. But I don't think features such as "hide all non-video participants" are essential to know about. Technology often needlessly holds people back from getting into the virtual speaking world as they overcomplicate it. I'm a big fan of keeping things as simple as possible in the beginning, then adding a more advanced technique or feature as time goes on.

Now that you know about some of the key features, in the next chapter, you are going to learn how to use them.

I.   Change views when appropriate
II. Get your audio crisp
III. Know both forms of recordings
IV. Use the abundance of interactive features

Chapter 23

One Zap, Two Zap, Many Zaps

After learning about the various features of Zoom, let's look at the versatile ways in which we can use them. Some of these ways may surprise you and will show you why Zoom has become my favourite tool of the last few years.

Solo

Although virtual speaking is all about transmitting your message to a global audience, the first way to use Zoom is solo. You can use some of the features that make it a great group tool for your own purposes. There are two ways in particular that I've found useful.

Recording Content

Although I usually advocate using a phone camera for filming solo videos, as the quality is higher, the webcam of course is where I first started. I wasn't aware of Zoom back then, so I used a default webcam app on my MacBook which wasn't as good. For anyone starting now, I'd tell them to go straight to Zoom.

Zoom does offer some advantages over the phone. The key aspect is screen sharing. If you want to record a presentation using slides, play a video, or instruct people on how to use a webpage or software, you will have great difficulty trying to do that on a phone. Zoom, on the other hand, does that simply. So if you want to record a video or even a webinar that needs those extra visual aspects, then Zoom is a better place to do it.

To prove this point, I recorded an entire online course "Get Zappy with Zoom" using just the Zoom app. It allowed me to speak direct-to-camera, but also to show slides on the screen, and screen share me navigating around the course homepage to show people how to access the content. You don't have to record an entire course using Zoom, but it's a great option to have at your disposal.

What I frequently use this function for now is recording my client's speech feedback. I'll have a PDF with "Cliffe Notes" on their speech on screen, then I will talk through it point by point. This allows me to demonstrate ideas on video, such as how they use a gesture or how to change the pacing of a part of their speech. I then send them the PDF file and the video file of the recording.

Practicing

The second way you can use Zoom solo is to practice. Considering that you will spend a lot of time presenting on Zoom, this is the perfect place to practice. Once again, using the recording feature, you can watch your performance back to assess and analyse. The video doesn't lie. You might think your body language is open, but the camera will show you when you are closing yourself off. You might think your articulation is clear, but when you have to turn the volume up to try and hear what you're saying, you'll realise you're mumbling.

I only started using this feature to practice over the last few years. Up until the pandemic, I had never seen Zoom as anything other than a video call tool for 1-1 conversations. So I used to practice my speeches by just walking around my office. It allowed me to practice my content, but not so much my delivery. I couldn't get that objective feedback on how I looked as I presented. Was emotion coming through my face or was it blank? Were my gestures congruent or scattered? Even for speeches you'll be delivering physically, I would still use this feature, as you don't truly know how you are performing until you capture it on camera.

Dual

After considering how to use Zoom as an individual, the next consideration is how to use it as a pair. This is how I was first introduced to Zoom back in 2018 because I used to it record...

Podcast Interviews

Zoom is probably the go-to platform for most podcasters, particularly small to medium-sized podcasts. It's certainly how I first came across it long before the pandemic made it a platform everyone was familiar with. The features of Zoom make this easy to do. You can use it to do a video interview, allowing you to see each other, read body language, and post the recording in both video and audio format. Or if you prefer audio only, you simply conduct the interview with the cameras off. You can record using the cloud, which allows you to interview people back to back. If you have more than one host or more than one guest, you can all connect remotely without having to gather in one studio.

Client Interviews

Although I have put my podcast on ice for the foreseeable future, there's one area where I am still utilising my podcast skills. Rather than using my interview skills for podcast guests, it's with my clients.

For my group programs, I like to catch up with each member 1-1 every 4 months to check in with how they are doing, find out what's working for them, and collect suggestions on how we can continue to improve their experience.

We do this on Zoom, which is handy firstly because I live nowhere near most of them! Secondly, with their permission, I record the interviews. This gives me the chance to watch it back again to remind myself of key points (particularly the feedback). With their permission, I also compile the footage of the good stuff they said: how much better they feel since joining the program; key insights and lightbulb moments; results like paid speaking gigs they've managed to acquire since joining the program. I use this footage as video testimonials in my marketing. Rather than getting stilted, scripted testimonials delivered solo, I get testimonials that are much more natural and conversational (and saying good stuff too!)

Group Use

This is perhaps where Zoom has earned its stripes throughout the pandemic and how most people got introduced to it. Therefore you might not have been aware of the solo and dual-use aspects of the platform! Even as you've sat on endless meetings for work or done quiz after quiz with friends and family, you may not have been using Zoom to its full potential. Let's explore the ways that Zoom can help you amplify your message.

Social/Networking

You already know about the social benefits of those endless quizzes, but have you thought about being more strategic about getting groups together on Zoom?

One of the projects that I implemented in my Facebook group during the pandemic was quarterly social events. It started with a one-off Christmas Quiz at the end of 2020 which proved so popular that it then grew into Easter Games, Summer Storytelling, and Halloween Dress-Up. It's difficult to build a community vibe in the Facebook group using just live videos and engagement in the comments, so these quarterly socials provide the opportunity to get to know some of the people in the group a little more closely. At these events we have a very "loose" public speaking theme and do some kind of activity centred around public speaking to provide a bit of structure but otherwise, I'm not "teaching" any material, we are just chatting and having fun

(I give some prizes out at the end which also makes people quite happy!).

Although I haven't attended such an event, as I'm averse to "networking" in its old-fashioned form, I do know of people who have run and attended popular networking events on Zoom. The networking uses breakout rooms and speed networking to form individual connections, and then pitches in the main room to reach a wider audience. This is something that you may wish to host or attend too if appropriate for your industry.

Workshop

I'll go as far as to say that if you are not currently running some kind of regular webinar or workshop on Zoom, do it now! It's such an easy, cost-effective way to build your speaking experience and reach a new audience. When I started out as a speaker I was speaking in coffee shops, bar basements, and community centres to try and cut my teeth. If I was starting today I would have begun on Zoom to refine my content before moving into the physical realm.

Even today, I run a "Virtual Speaking Masterclass" on the 25th of every month (except December!) and have anywhere between 40-80 people in attendance. The feedback for these sessions is positive, I get to meet people from around the world, and some of the attendees end up joining one of my paid programs later down the line. I run the same content each time so there's little prep time now. I just show up for 90 minutes, have fun, meet new people and answer some questions.

After outlining each of those ways to use Zoom, in the next chapter we are going to take a deeper dive into that final use we discussed. You're going to learn the key skills of running workshops on Zoom, and some best practices to think about to ensure the best audience experience.

I. *Record and practice by yourself*
II. *Interview others*
III. *Bring more people into the revolution*

Chapter 24

Working The Room

In your virtual speaking career, you are going to find yourself in many virtual rooms. Knowing best practices for these scenarios is key to your success virtually, and why people will be quite happy to experience you virtually even when a physical opportunity is not available.

To Sit Or Stand

This first consideration might surprise you because perhaps you haven't even thought about standing. We're so used to sitting down at our desk to be on Zoom, I was the same! At the start of the pandemic, I was sitting at my desk and looking down at my screen (all the things I tell you not to do!). Then I attended our very first virtual Toastmasters Zoom meeting and one of our club members, Lauren, broke the early established mould when she stood to deliver her speech. All of her passion, energy, and playfulness that I had seen in her physical speeches transferred to the online format. That's when I realised that standing to speak was a serious option that needed to be considered.

Let's examine some of the reasons why standing to speak is so effective, and the times that it might still be more advantageous to sit.

Stand

The biggest factor in standing to speak is energy. Speaking whilst standing makes you a lot more dynamic, it allows for bigger and broader gestures and you can move around your speaking area more like a physical stage. Standing (especially if everyone else is sitting) also grants you more presence and authority.

Moreover, when we sit, we generally have bad posture. We slump, which makes our gestures smaller and reduces our presence. It also constricts our ribcage, making us breathe less efficiently and this, in turn, damages our voice. Have you noticed after a long day of speaking on Zoom your voice is hoarse? That is due, in part, to inefficient breathing. That isn't solved completely by standing, but it is mitigated considerably.

Therefore, I recommend standing whenever you have a high-stakes speaking engagement: like a pitch to investors or a keynote at a large conference. It will give you more authority and energy when you present. If you are speaking for a long time, anything over 30 minutes really, then you may want to consider standing to protect your voice.

So is standing always the best option? Not necessarily.

Sit

Picture this scenario. You're in the office (physically) and your boss calls you into a team meeting. You all sit around the conference table, but your boss stands and speaks to you here for the entire duration. How do you feel?

It's a little intimidating, right? It feels like you're being berated, lectured, and talked down to. Even if your boss is being civil, you wonder what the power play here is.

That scenario translates to online, there are times when standing may create that inappropriate power dynamic. It's fine for a workshop, but not for a meeting. Additionally, there may be times when you want to intentionally soften yourself, even if standing wouldn't necessarily be intimidating.

If you are wanting to create a relaxed, conversational environment, then you would be better served sitting. Imagine you are bringing together a new team for the first time, or you are wanting to encourage lots of participation in a workshop. If you are sitting, then it won't look like you are putting yourself on a pedestal and people will automatically relax around you.

I mix it up between standing and sitting. I stand when I want more presence and dynamism, and sit when I want more informality and participation.

Screen Switching

The worst thing you can do as a speaker is have your screen sharing from the moment a Zoom call starts, and keep it on for the entire duration of the session. If you think back to the active window principle from many chapters ago, this doesn't create an active window. It's the slow trawl of slide after slide, usually packed with text and read in a monotonous drawl.

Even if you have minimal slides and an engaging voice, audiences do get stuck in passive, consumer mode when you present in this style, rather than being active participants.

Frequent interactive opportunities can certainly help with this, and we'll cover those next in the chapter. But another way to keep your audience's attention is simply to not get stuck on the slides for too long.

You can use slides to demonstrate a key visual, then stop the screen share and come back into the room to encourage some participation. You then might want to cover the next section with cue cards rather than slides, then return to the slides for the following section, then come back into the gallery view for audience participation. This back-and-forth keeps the audience on their toes and stops them from getting sucked into passive slide viewer mode and thinking about drifting into their email inboxes and WhatsApp messages.

Interaction

We've touched upon interactive techniques throughout this book. It's one of the most important parts of speaking in general, and possibly even more so on virtual. As well as touching upon some familiar ground, we're also going to look in more detail at some of the best practice for interacting on Zoom.

Verbal Answers

The best way to simulate being in a physical room with people is to have them speak, not type. Ignore all the interactive tools for a moment and just consider how you can get your audience to speak. Ask them to unmute and contribute. When you ask questions, get people to shout out answers. When you get your audience to do a reflective written exercise, get them to share their answers with the group. Get them to do verbal tasks and activities (I do this a lot when I'm teaching public speaking for obvious reasons!).

With a small group, I rarely do any other type of interaction, but that's the key phrase: a small group. Getting people to shout out soon becomes untenable. I'm comfortable doing this style of interaction with up to about 20-25 people. After that, it can become a little congested and you may need to move on to the virtual tools.

Chat Box

This feature has become one of my best friends on Zoom. It allows you to maintain a two-way dialogue with the audience even when the mute buttons are on. You can use it to ask questions and collect answers, and the audience can use it to ask you questions too.

As much as I love it, the chat box does have its limits. If you ask a question that requires a short answer (e.g. yes or no), even with a smaller audience, those answers can come through rapidly and make it difficult to read and keep track of them. This is okay if you are just looking for a stream of reassuring "yeses" (for example, "can you see my slides?"), but if you are trying to parse information from your audience, this might be more challenging.

With a little bit of tact and patience, the chat box is still an effective tool up to anywhere from 100 to 200 people, depending on how engaged your audience is (some people will never type in the chat no matter how many questions you ask). Eventually, you will reach a point where those chat answers just come in too fast for you to process them effectively during your presentation. Then you may have to consider alternative options.

Polls

Polls work much better than the chat box for collecting information quickly from a large group. If I was speaking to a large group of hundreds of people on Zoom, Rather than asking a question like "Have you ever been paid to speak? Type yes or no in the chat box" and trying to count the flurry of answers coming in, I can just make a poll and get people to "vote" for their answer. It won't take people long and I will quickly get feedback that tells me whether the majority of the audience has or has not been paid to speak.

Don't feel that polls are restricted to large audiences either. You can use polls with a smaller audience not just to collect information but to guide your presentation. For example, you might ask "what area of business do you feel you struggle with most: design, marketing, or sales?" Depending on what answer comes through, you can then tailor your next piece of content to focus on that key area and make it more useful to the audience in front of you. You might deliver that presentation multiple times, but you can also tailor it to your audience depending on what their needs are so they don't feel you are just delivering a generic presentation to them.

Breakout Rooms

One of the considerations that has emerged from how we use interactive tools is the audience size. One tool you have to manipulate the audience size is Breakout Rooms. Imagine you have an audience of 50 – that is too high for doing verbal contributions – but if you make 10 rooms of 5 people, then they can make verbal contributions within those rooms.

What you have to be mindful of with breakout rooms is how they are regulated. For a relatively simple task or activity, you can stay in one room whilst everyone else gets divided up and trust that everyone will be able to complete it comfortably. If it is more complex, or the groups are larger (generally double figures), then you may want a facilitator in the room. Do you do that by yourself, shifting from room to room without being able to focus on one? Or do you have multiple facilitators who are on hand to be assigned to each room? If you going to have over 100 people in the audience, are you realistically going to have enough people to help you facilitate, or the work done in the breakout rooms be productive? These are issues that become increasingly difficult to address.

Breakout Rooms can help you increase the feasibility of verbal interaction in larger audiences, but even then you will probably only be able to stretch this so far. Breakout Rooms can work well in audiences up to 50-75, but after that, they become quite difficult to execute.

With these extra nuances in mind, you now have everything you need to start running successful Zoom events.

I.   *Stand for the Revolution*
II.   *Switch it up*
III. *Utilise all the interactive tools*

It Is Declared!

Deliver With Zeal

Zoom became one of the words of the year in 2020. In this declaration, we've explored how to make it one of your words of the year, every year.

You've learned how to navigate all the various features of Zoom so that you don't get tripped up by the tech and can identify the few buttons you need to focus on.

Next, you learned how versatile Zoom is and how to use it whether you are alone, with one person, or with many people.

Finally, we explored some of the considerations of delivering on Zoom, to ensure that you deliver in a way that is engaging and makes people forget there is even a difference between physical and virtual speaking.

The Revolution is about to begin.

Viva La Revolution

How One Woman Revolutionised Her Speaking

On the 1st of April, 2020, I started the Rise and Inspire Speakers Facebook group. I didn't yet know exactly how this was going to look, but one thing I knew was that I wanted it to be a place that gave speakers opportunities. So I decided that every month, we would run a virtual summit called "Inspire Week". For a 7-day period, any member could sign up for a 30-minute speaking slot to go live to the rest of the group. I assigned rough themes to each day to help prompt our speakers to think of topics to speak on.

We ran our first event from Monday 20th to Sunday 26th of April. We had about 25 people speak and, unbeknownst to me, five of those people would become my first public speaking clients.

These are some of the names you've heard already. Sara who wanted to speak about being bipolar but took two attempts to speak up about it in the group. Jenn who whispers to the camera. David visiting his sister for Christmas (he didn't deliver this speech in April of course!). Then there was Ije.

Ije had been invited into the group by a friend, who said it might be a good place to raise awareness of her charity. In her first Inspire Week speech, Ije told us how she had grown up in

Nigeria before living in the UK for the last ten years. She told us of the terrorist group Buka Haram and the devastation they caused to families. She told us of the orphanage she ran to try and help child survivors of the atrocities.

I saw that Ije had a good manner of speaking. She was confident but also relaxed. However, her speaking technique was all over the place. She wasn't looking at the camera. There were few gestures. She hadn't turned her phone onto "Do Not Disturb" so notifications were pinging throughout her speech. The speech was informative without being punchy, there wasn't really a clear purpose or message to it. I saw she had a lot of potential but would require some guidance to realise it.

When I decided to test a group coaching program with five clients, Ije was one of the five who came on board. The biggest compliment I can pay Ije is that she soaked up every suggestion and piece of feedback like a sponge. When she delivered her first speech as a client, I gave her feedback on all the points of technique I had noted in her first speech. The next time she spoke, she was looking at the camera, using gestures and getting a clearer purpose to her speaking. When I gave her feedback on how to structure her speeches more coherently, I saw her employ it straight away.

We were halfway through this three-month group coaching program when George Floyd was murdered. As a black woman who had spent the last ten years living in the predominantly white U.K., Ije had a lot of anecdotes, lessons, and messages to share on the topic of racism and diversity.

In our June Inspire Week, just our third such event in the Facebook group, we had a Black Lives Matter day. Thursday the 25th of June was reserved just for speakers of colour to talk about the variety of issues that George Floyd's murder had thrown up. Ije delivered a speech entitled "The Power of an Idea", demonstrating that Black Lives Matter was an idea whose time had come. She used parables, imagery, and metaphor to bring the subject to life using all her newly acquired delivery skills.

It was a speech that got shared far beyond the group and was picked up and featured on the official Black Lives Matter UK website. She received a request to speak for an organisation and they offered her £300 ($400) to deliver the speech again for them. This became the first of many speaking engagements for Ije.

Ije and I worked together for 6 months in total. By the end of 2020, she was ready to go off on her own and started to speak for some of the biggest names in the UK: the NHS, HMRC, HM Prison's Service, The Prince's Trust, and many more. I would get frequent messages from Ije. "You'll never guess who's asked me to speak" and "You'll never believe how much they've offered to pay me." One of Ije's most recent messages at the time of writing is that she got paid £750 ($1000) to speak for 30 minutes at a college. In about 18 months her rate has gone from £300 an hour to £1500 an hour (£750 for 1/2 hour). We've even had the chance to speak together at the same event. What's even more amazing is that she has done all this as a single mum, still working her full-time job, and running her charity at the same time.

Ije's journey demonstrates that when you understand the techniques of virtual speaking and employ them correctly and consistently, they pay off. Her rise was particularly rapid and I'm not saying you'll see magic in 6 months, but you will see significant progress in that time.

Ije has essentially created a new career for herself with virtual speaking. It has opened more opportunities for her in her career. It has created greater exposure for her charity. It gives her the flexibility to work around her parenting duties. She is one of the key examples of how virtual speaking opens up new opportunities for not just our work, but the rest of our lives too.

As you've read this book, there may have been a nagging thought at the back of your mind. As you've read the vignettes about people using virtual speaking during the pandemic, as you've thought about the skills required on camera, the question you've been thinking to yourself is.

"What happens when the pandemic is over?"

The necessity for virtual speaking came about because we had to work from home and isolate ourselves as much as possible. Now that it seems the worst of COVID-19 is behind us, isn't it time to get back in front of people, and the skills for speaking on camera are no longer necessary?

The first point I'll make in response is that we can't possibly predict the future. Even in January 2020 few people (myself included) really took the threat of COVID-19 seriously. Pandemics were a thing of the past right? Yet just two months later COVID-19 really knocked us off our feet, even with our modern medicine and technological adaptations. It's been tough, but thank goodness it wasn't like the Black Death wiping out the populations of countries around the world by a third or even a half. We can't be complacent about future pandemics and virtual solutions will be required again as part of our strategy to fight them if (when) we encounter them again.

Didn't we also think we were done with wars in Europe? Again us Europeans were complacent that wars were something that happened "elsewhere". Just when we are starting to see the other side of COVID-19, Russia invades Ukraine, creating new fears and challenges around security and energy. Again in January 2022, I don't think many of us thought there would be Russian boots on Ukrainian soil by March.

We can't predict what other challenges will arise this decade, but I will bet one thing. They are going to happen. I know this sounds pessimist, but anticipating challenges will help us better prepare for them. Virtual communication is a meta-skill this decade and I hope this century. It gives you more options when things get tough. Look at how President Zelensky of Ukraine has managed to rally support and forge alliances using virtual means. Let's hope that we don't find ourselves a wartime leader, but the ability to effectively communicate is always a way to help get yourself out of trouble. It gives you the ability to jump ship from a collapsed industry, build more job security for yourself, and earn extra income on the side. In an increasingly chaotic and unpredictable world, virtual communication skills provide you with a source of stability and security.

The second point is more optimistic. We actually found benefits in virtual work. The toothpaste is out of the tube with virtual speaking. We've seen that people don't need to commute to the office just to sit in meetings when they can do that at home. We've seen that people don't have to fly around the world for conferences when we can host them remotely. We've seen that the only way to effectively work across oceans and time zones is with virtual communication.

The future is hybrid. Sometimes physical is the best option, but sometimes virtual is. If I could make one final argument for the importance of virtual speaking, it would be this. Virtual speaking isn't about building work skills. It's about building more freedom in your life. The virtual option is about having the freedom to choose. When your child is sick, it gives you the choice to stay at home with them without missing out on the work required to provide for them. When you work shifts, it means that there is always someone awake in the world to listen to your live stream videos. When you live in the middle of nowhere, it allows you to tap into the opportunities of the big cities.

Virtual speaking is an equaliser. All you need is a camera and an internet connection to reach people around the world. After that, it's all down to your ability to communicate. In this book, you have learned what you can do to develop these skills and be a part of this new way of doing things. The Revolution has begun. Are you going to join?

The Virtual Speakers Revolution Declaration

Declaration One: Build Your Movement

Declaration Two: Be Charismatic On Camera

Declaration Three: Thrive On Live

Declaration Four: Be YOU-nique On Youtube

Declaration Five: Get Zappy With Zoom

Join The Revolutionary Movement

Rate and Review

Ratings and reviews are the lifeblood of independent revolutionary authors such as myself! If you enjoyed this book, please tell others why you enjoyed it with an Amazon review.

Virtual Connection

As stressed so much in this book, we can stay in touch from anywhere in the world. Here are some of the best ways to do that:

Website: www.davidmccrae.net
Facebook Group: Rise and Inspire Speakers (RAIS)
Youtube: David McCrae: Virtual Speaking Coach
Linkedin: David McCrae: Virtual Speaking Coach

Virtual Speakers Club

In the VSC we meet every two weeks online to develop our virtual speaking skills and make friends around the world. Here's a breakdown of how we do it:

1) Educational Workshop

The first part of each meeting will be a workshop delivered by me where you will learn:

- The key tenets of public speaking so that you know how to structure your speeches, tell engaging stories and be able to prepare for any speech at short notice.
- Which techniques help you appear and feel confident, hold your audience's attention, and inspire them to take action on your message.
- What tricks you can use with technology to create more engaging speeches, unite large groups of people, and establish yourself as an expert in your industry.

2) Speeches and Evaluation

In the second part of the meeting, members will take turns delivering a 10-minute speech and get an evaluation from everyone in the club. This will allow you to:

- Identify weak areas to sharpen your skills as a speaker.
- Practice important content to get it just right before you deliver it for real.
- Allow you to experiment with new material in a safe, supportive environment.

Additionally, every 12 weeks we will have a Networking Party. This is a meeting dedicated to building connections with each other so that you can:

• Make friends with like-minded people from across the world.
• Find out about new opportunities to speak and serve.
• Create partnerships that allow you to increase your impact and income.

Learn more about how joining can improve your virtual speaking skills by visiting: https://davidmccrae.thinkific.com/courses/virtual-speakers-club

Acknowledgements

Spending a lot of time isolating in your house makes you appreciate a lot of things: fresh air, home delivery, internet streaming, and reasonably priced handwash. Undoubtedly the thing it made us all appreciate most though was people. The people who we were lucky enough to be with during lockdown, and the people we could only stay connected with virtually.

The first person was the one I was locked up with for all those months: my wife Kerrie. Six months before lockdown we said "until death do us part" at the wedding altar. We didn't think being locked in the house together was going to be part of the marriage deal! I would have gone crazy without her with me as we created Zoom quiz questions, steamrolled our way through TV shows, experimented with new recipes, and had our lunch breaks together. COVID proved to me that there is no one else I would want to spend my life locked up with.

I also appreciate the amazing work of my therapist Wendy Li, who helped me sort out the mess my head was in at the start of 2020, even when the madness of COVID was going on. She is seriously impressive at work.

I'm thankful to the friends and family who kept us sane during that time. Jamie, Roz, Andrew, and Lauren who we did a weekly Zoom quiz with. All of Kerrie's family who we did another weekly quiz with! Jess and Styli who were the first friends we saw when we were able to see people outside our household. Kerrie's parents who were the first people we saw when we were able to travel again.

I'm grateful for all the friends we went walking with when we were still being cautious: Josh, Jamie and Sarah, David, Viktor, Edward, and apologies to anyone I missed in the flurry of dog walks in the woods and grabbing coffees in the park. I've been delighted to work with some amazing people around the world during this time and I think I've learned more from them than they will ever learn from me: Sara Mathis, Jenn Walter, Ije McDougall, David Martin, Michelle Foulia, Leah Kitoloh, Wendy Phillips, Lisa Dimino White, Raychel Paterson, Zerah Muhaji, Krystle Dookoo, Julie Paulston, Mulugeta Asgedom, Sunny Parmar, Isis Leeor, Imogen Brown, Morag Gardner, Maryanne Wilson Co, and Melanie Leamy. There are many more virtual friends I've made during this time that would be hard to list completely.

During this period, I've had unprecedented access to mentoring and feedback around the world to help me with my speaking, writing, and coaching. Some of the people I'd like to thank in this regard are Kyle Murtagh, James McGinty, Chris Murphy, David Martin (coaching is a two-way street!), Viktor Saghy, Alex Kidd, Gudrun Hoehne, Paul O'Mahony, May Wong, Jamie Corrales, Andrew Horberry, Stephan Dyer, Irmine Roshim, Craig Curtis, Claire Wright, and Mark Carolan.

A special note of appreciation goes to Karen Yates, who we lost right at the start of my journey described in this book. She mentored me a lot when I was struggling with Author Your Life and is always shining a light on me in my new career with her halo light.

Thank you also to Oleksandra Den for the cover design. I wanted to convey the future without looking dystopian, and bring in ideas of revolution without looking fascist or communist. I think she managed to strike the balance well. I hope you agree.

My final note of gratitude is, as with every book, to you. Firstly to reward you if you have read all the way through these acknowledgements. Secondly, because I would have no book to write any acknowledgements in if it wasn't for you supporting my writing by buying books, telling friends and family about them, and posting about the book on social media. However much I have helped you by writing this book, you have helped me far more by reading it. I would have never gotten to my sixth book if it wasn't for every reader who has supported my writing. Thank you for supporting this book.

About The Author

David was born in Aberdeen, Scotland, to an English mum and a Scottish dad. He jokes that this makes him a Half-Blood, just like Harry Potter. He was raised in the village of Banchory just outside Aberdeen. Arguably the village's biggest claim to fame is that the Queen of the United Kingdom drives through it every time she stays in her Balmoral Estate in the Cairngorm National Park.

David was a nerd long before it was cool to be one. David has watched the Lord of the Rings films over 100 times and used to own a replica sword from the movies, which will naturally be replaced with a lightsaber when they get invented. He is taking on the challenge of consuming all the new Star Wars content Disney+ can churn out. David knows, as any intelligent person does, that Han shot first.

After growing up in Scotland and watching the Lord of the Rings on repeat, it's unsurprising that David has developed a fondness for mountains and is currently working his way through the Scottish Munros: the 282 mountains over 3000 ft tall in the country. He's over halfway through and on the countdown.

David is a long-suffering fan of Scottish Rugby. Every year he sits down eagerly to watch the Six Nations Championship and hopes this year will be the year that Scotland wins their first title (the lights of the false dawn are getting very familiar).

David also has a minor obsession with cats. He speaks to the cats in his neighbourhood and has assigned them all names and personalities. Some of the cats reciprocate his attention. All of his neighbours give him a wide berth. After years of surrogate cats, he finally has a kitty in the home, a middle-aged rescue called Isla who likes lots of cuddles and snacks.

David likes to consider himself a "Pun Master". He knows the double-meaning of far too many words and will jump upon any opportunity to showcase that knowledge. His personal favourite is when he went to a restaurant and a waiter greeted him with a tray of drinks.

"Aperitif?" the waiter asked.

"No thanks," David said, pointing to his mouth, "I've already got a set."

This is another reason David likes Virtual Speaking. When he tells a bad joke, he can assume everyone is laughing.

Printed in Great Britain
by Amazon

15736597R00132